Painting in Waldorf Education

Painting in Waldorf Education

by
Dick Bruin
and
Attie Lichthart

Waldorf
PUBLICATIONS

Printed with support from the Waldorf Curriculum Fund

Published by:

Waldorf Publications at the
Research Institute for Waldorf Education
38 Main Street
Chatham, NY 12037

Title: *Painting in Waldorf Education*
Authors: Dick Bruin and Attie Lichthart
Translator: Paula Helder
Editor: David Mitchell
Proofreader: Ann Erwin
Cover: Hallie Wootan

ISBN# 978-1-936367-79-5
Revised 2015

First published in 1994
Second edition (revised) 2000 by Vrij Pedagogisch Centrum
with the title: *Schilderen op School*

Foreword

Painting in Waldorf Education came to the attention of AWSNA Publications through the attentiveness and courtesy of Peter and Tjitske Lehmann, colleagues from the Kimberton Waldorf School, to whom we express our gratitude.

For some time we have been searching for a comprehensive book on painting through the curriculum, and we believe that this title will be of benefit to all English-speaking Waldorf teachers and parents.

The uniqueness of watercolor painting as a significant component of child development requires understanding and study. This effort comes from two seasoned Waldorf teachers, Attie Lichthart and Dick Bruin from Holland, who do an admirable job providing sound reasoning, practical advice, clear exercises for teachers, and beautiful examples. It is also appropriate that this work originates from Dutch colleagues, the home country of so many master painters.

We hope that this book serves you well.

– David Mitchell
AWSNA Publications

Contents

3. High School

4. Additional Aspects for the Didactics of the Painting Lesson

1. Painting in Education

The Discovery
When you look
Around you
You'll see that
Everything has color.
– K. Schippers

1.1 Introduction

A child's land is a land of color. Children are surrounded all day by colors. Only darkness can make the world of color disappear; color only becomes visible with the light. Initially the child experiences how colors in nature undergo major changes in the course of the year. The same each year. Out of the grey sombre winter spring colors appear: first the fresh spring green, then the colorful flowers, a pink glow in the budding beech forest. Heavier and darker are the greens around us when spring gives way to summer. Children pick flowers along the roadside and in the meadows. Wild flowers cover the wayside. Gardens become a profusion of color experience. Each child has a preference for a particular color or flower. When autumn comes along, things become even more interesting. New, often clear and warm colors spark up from tree or shrub. Before the leaf falls and the plants give themselves up to the earth, they show the fruit of the warm summer sun one more time in yellow, red, orange and brown.

The activities which so far have taken place above the soil now move inwards, into the earth, into the soil itself. Colors also withdraw and the form element, i.e., the shape of the tree itself, takes their place. Bare branches are set sharply against the chill autumn sky. Playing outside is over. Everyone withdraws into their houses. Now children experience the color impressions inside the house. Particularly in our time we come across the most fantastic colors in furnishings, on the walls and floors, ranging from soft pastel hues to brightly and vividly dyed fabrics. Colors are indeed present everywhere you look. Inside and outside. In the past few years colors have also popped up in children's fashion with lively, flowery and striped designs. It breathes complete zest for life. Prints from all over the world can be seen on dresses, blouses and trousers. Everything can be combined. A wonderful time for children in which color is so widespread and present in fashion, home and environment.

The day itself has its own color nuances. The red or orange morning sky. Jet black, threatening thunderclouds or a blue sky, out of which you could cut a sailor's uniform. What child would not stop to consider the red glowing sunrise or would not hope to find a pot of gold at the end of the rainbow, which, (especially in our [Dutch] landscape) in the low beam of a light set against the dark clouds, and the slightly mysterious way the moon places houses and surroundings in a pale light.

Playing with light is fun too. Where there's light, shadow often can be found. Shadow tag is a favorite game with long shadows of small friends. Slightly older children are able to start experiencing that shadows can be colored. As children grow older, new color experiences continually arise, in particular, during the holidays, when the country's borders are crossed. Especially in the Netherlands, because of the flat landscape, we can see so much sky, the countryside is especially highlighted. This gives rise to many experiences with regard to light. Through the centuries painters have lauded our country for this quality. Clouds, rain and mist, which play a constantly varying game with seawind and light, give our climate a fresh and lively tint. In and among this quality Dutch children live their daily lives. To a lesser or greater degree of awareness they absorb the colors. They are inspired by them and wish to start working with them. For all the children in the world playing with colors is a favorite game, depending on the character of their environment. This daily environment strongly influences both play at home and at school. Learning is a game. Playing with colors becomes a learning process, daily experiences expressed in the language of colors. In this process both parent and teacher provide helping hands. This workbook has been written for them.

1.2 Colors and their effects on people

So, everything around us has color. The blue sky, the golden yellow corn, the grey terraced houses, the pink blossom. We live submerged in a bath of colors. And just as when lying in a bath we know that our bodies contain a large percentage of water, we can equally imagine that the colorful life around us also takes place within the human being. The younger the child, the more transparent the skin indicating the separation between outer and inner world. Colors affect our feeling life. Whether you like it or not colors call on us, by way of our observation, our senses. Colors can greatly influence or "color" our moods. On the other hand we express ourselves with the colors we choose for clothing, interiors or works of art. In this way, by means of color, we set up a lively dialogue with the outside world.

In *Spirituality and Abstraction in Art* Wassily Kandinsky (1866–1944) says the following about color, artist and painting: "In general, in this way, color is a means of directly influencing the soul. Color is the key. The eye is the hammer. The soul is the many stringed grand piano. The artist is the hand playing this or that key consciously causing the vibration of the human soul." Kandinsky's work led to "Seelengemalde" [soul painting], to an abstract expression which was no longer inspired by the reality of visible nature, but by one's inner feelings.

Children being more susceptible in general are consequently more sensitive to colors. For example, an overcast grey sky when opening the bedroom curtains can sometimes set the mood for the rest of the day. In a colorful lush summer meadow children can go wild with fun. These are extremes examples of course, but they show the obvious powerful workings of color in any environment. The youngest children always like to pick out the most brightly colored toy. In a manner of speaking, they become one with the color. They inwardly "color" themselves constantly to their surroundings. One child may feel comfortable with a particular color, whereas another child may be adversely affected by it. In adults these forces are less strong. We are less open to this in our daily lives and can shut ourselves off to a degree. Adults have thicker skins. What the child observes (including color) has a direct effect on the working and shaping of the body. Color influences the way in which the observation is absorbed by the body. Rudolf Steiner points out that even our metabolism can be stimulated by a correct development of the sight organ through color and light. We also know that our appetite is linked to the color of our dishes. Who fancies blue pudding? In this way a link is established between health, food and color. Color, as therapy, is seriously researched and applied. We can find directions as to the workings of color on a child at the change of teeth in *The Education of the Child* by Rudolf Steiner.

> An excited child, referred to as a nervous child, should be treated differently with regard to his environment than a lethargic, inactive child. Here everything should be considered, from the colors of the room and its contents to the clothes the child wears. An excited child should be surrounded by red or orange colors and dressed in these colors. Conversely, a passive child should have blue and blue green colors in its environment. These contrasting colors are important, because they are awakened internally.[1]

Red's complementary color is green, blue's is orange-yellow. This contrasting color is produced by the physical organs of the child and establishes a structure within it, corresponding with this color, which is necessary to the child.

After their ninth year, as children become more distanced with regard to their outer environment and further develop their inner world, the influence of color will acquire a different character. The complementary effect diminishes in adults, and color observation becomes stronger. Red activates and green brings peace. Dealing with these trends requires loving gifts of observation from the educator.

1.3 The task of the teacher

A fast-changing world increasingly places changing demands upon us. The minute we feel we have mastered one new development, another new one follows. Many inventions in the field of technology, for example, are incomprehensible to the layman. In this way one

1. Steiner, Rudolf. *Soul Economy in Waldorf Education*. First lecture, New York: Anthroposophic Press, 1986.

may get the feeling of constantly trying to catch up with things. As a result one is inclined to close his eyes to such matters. Dealing with all these external impressions with their resulting inner reactions is not easy. The extremes are far removed from each other and evoke a great tension. How do I find a balance? Each of us will recognize these inner processes.

As individuals we are equally built up from polar forces. On the one side we join with our bodies the line of the realm of nature, next to the plant and mineral world; on the other hand we have great ideals, wishes and expectations that spring from our spiritual origins. Impulses which bear down upon us from both these poles are taken up and united by the soul. The soul is shaped from these things, which are our ideals. It is fed by this as well as by the creative force arising from our will. The soul becomes polarized. The balance is developed by our feeling life. Physically this is expressed through rhythmic breathing, where there is a constant link between internal and external. The heart and circulation also connect top and bottom. An idea which has formed into a clear image through our thinking, we can apply concretely in practice through our enthusiasm (to warm to something), by means of our will (i.e., our hands). On the other hand action can occur unconsciously, initiated externally, so to speak: we are enthused by something, which can eventually lead to and idea or thought. In this way many a notion enters our thinking life, which we can then deal with consciously. This always concerns two areas. The feeling life builds a bridge between these essentially differing qualities: thinking and acting.

This soul world, in which the three soul qualities of thinking, feeling, and willing function independently yet together, is still a small world in the young child. The soul expands as it processes more experiences. Through new actions, feelings, and thoughts the soul matures. In the thinking and willing field the tension lies between distance and repetitions, between creativity and training. When the natural lively interaction taking place in the soul is brought to a standstill causing the three soul qualities to become isolated, stress and fear will take possession of the soul. In a manner of speaking the head will no longer know what the hand or foot is doing. Ideas remain unrealized ideals. Feelings are suppressed or bottled up. At a later stage an individual may become unreachable and show apathy. The distance between the inner life and the outer world increases. Soon the soul is no longer able to build a connection. In contrast, a healthy development of the soul always creates unity. Qualities can develop that help to provide an answer to external questions and internal questions.

Art, specifically, gives us the opportunity to support and stimulate soul development, for it is in this field that all three soul qualities are addressed by means of creativity. By creating, enthusiasm is initiated. Out of this new ideas develop. Once an image is there to be worked out, the feeling weighs up what needs to be done. Then the necessary actions round off the original idea. Essentially all forms of art follow this path.

What place does painting occupy next to form-drawing and clay modeling? With form-drawing capturing the movement is the main goal: a big or small movement made specially with hand, foot or the whole body. A downstroke expressed in a line is the essence of form-drawing. The line as a solidified movement. In other words: the path of the movement. This interplay of lines takes place in a one-dimensional world. The line becomes clearly visible, contrasting with the paper background. This is why one can use dark tints of crayon (chalk) or pencil in form-drawing. Color plays no part in this field. The eye must be given the opportunity to follow the movement, freely without obstructions. We prefer to describe the subject with verbs, rather than nouns, which anchor the movement too much and often call up fixed images. The words "fall asleep" or "wake up" give a pupil more space than the word "spiral." We're talking about an inward movement and subsequent outward movement. Verbs tend to stress the process, the road traveled in that time.

With painting we enter into the two-dimensional world. Depth is created by the different effects of color. Colors create space, not through an interplay of light and darkness, but through pure color effect. The term "color perspective" is appropriate here. A certain training of the eye is required to consider paintings from this angle. We are too often tempted by the quick success of interplay between lines and light (darkness) to suggest spaces. Amongst the classical modern painters of the twentieth century many examples of color perspective can be found. They fought for a new way of thinking and rejected the old traditions. The paintings became "flatter" and consequently the color interplay became more prominent. The almost physically palpable spaces gave way to new and alternative representations of reality. Vanishing points, fixed composition schemes no longer played a part in this. When looking at the artist Cezanne, we can observe how painted objects free themselves from their environment through use of color. They seem to release themselves from gravity, thus creating a new reality in a different dimension.

Steiner stresses the uniqueness of painting as follows:

Deeper insight into colors has somehow dissipated and the artistic approach nowadays has given way to a falsified plastic approach. Nowadays we prefer to paint plastic (moldable) three dimensional people onto the canvas. With that aim, the spatial perspective has been developed (which actually emerged in the fifth post-Atlantean epoch) and which with the perspective line obviates that one aspect is more in the background and the other more in the foreground, meaning it wants to bring out spatial forms on the canvas. This rejects at the outset the most important material the artist has, for he does not create in space, he creates on a flat surface and it is quite ridiculous to want to experience the thing spatially when one's basic material is flat.[2]

Art which genuinely needs physical space in which to manifest itself is sculpture. Clay modeling and plastic art is a world of front and back, right and left, top and bottom. Space is explored by the sculpture and in its turn the sculpture lends itself to space. We can observe a sculpture from different angles.

In the Waldorf curriculum we notice that with these three different ways of dealing with space, through lines, color and image, three separate courses of study have been developed: the form-drawing, painting, and clay modeling plan. In the higher classes and at secondary level these directions can of course blend in all possible ways. For the first few years it is important to separate these three areas and to be aware in which field the teacher finds him/herself with the pupil. Each field responds to a special need and reflects an artistic process in its own way. Therefore, it is important to be alert when using color in form-drawing, when setting up areas of painting and when clay modeling.

When these three fields are dealt with clearly, pupils will be less inclined during form-drawing to fill up areas with color or to start drawing with a brush. Combining painting and drawing can be

---

2. See Steiner's *Art as Seen in the Light of Mystery Wisdom*, London: Rudolf Steiner Press, 1984.

very suitable for certain purposes; however, in the weekly recurring lesson it is important to explore the one-, two- and three-dimensional worlds first and to discover all possibilities.

1.4 Goethe's theory of color

Goethe, the great teacher in the field of living processes in nature, places our eye in the center of his argument about color. He states:

> Color is an elementary natural phenomenon intended
> for the sense of sight, which manifests itself, just like
> all others, through separation and contrast, through
> mingling and unification, through intensification
> and division and is best observed and understood in
> relation to these general natural fomulae.

Goethe sees the world of color originate from the actions of and the obstructions to light. In doing so he constructs an entire world out of light, darkness and obscured atmosphere, a threefold world with color in the center. Between light and darkness color comes into being. In his physics we constantly find the concepts of metamorphosis, polarity and intensification (*Steigerung*). With this he expresses processes occurring beyond the visible world, which do however determine the eventual manifestation.

Goethe distinguished only two pure colors: blue and yellow. They are polarized, meaning that with pure yellow it is impossible for blue to be present and vice versa. This discovery results from observing what happens when a turbid medium moves in front of the light, respectively a lit-up medium in front of darkness. When obscurity occurs before the light a yellow/red color is established in front of darkness. A blue-like violet color is established in front of darkness. This blue color can be seen daily in the atmosphere; the blue of the sky, when the sunlit earth atmosphere slides before the black universe. The yellow/red we can detect from the sun, when its light is mildly obscured during the day due to the atmosphere and more strongly during sunrise and sunset. Yellow, orange and red consequently come about as an activity of light in darkness, blue as a working of darkness in light.

These two elementary phenomena are the principles of Goethe's theory of color. Through the intensification of both processes yellow-red and blue-red come into being. When these two shine onto each other purple arises. When blue and yellow are mixed the color green is formed, thus closing the circle. This color circle arises from processes and is an expression of living forces. We will consider this in more detail in Chapter 6.

Goethe's starting point is that darkness is as great a reality as light. Light is only the result of objects being lit up and then being observed by us. In the discovery of Goethe's elemental phenomena, Steiner found confirmation of the notion of polarities in nature as well as in humans. All living creatures take their course through opposites. These opposites need to be balanced constantly. Steiner goes even further in describing darkness, color, and light as spiritual beings, at the basis of all phenomena in the field of the physical, the soul life and the spirituality of the human. In the above order three separate forces are at work: light, darkness and the creation of balance. The threefold notion can also be found with Aristotle. With red-yellow, light dominates the darkness. With blue-violet darkness dominates light. And with green both are kept in balance. Goethe rightly says: "My theory of color is as old as the world itself." His insight into nature forges a bridge between self-knowledge and world-knowledge.

With Goethe the importance is in how he made his observations and drew his conclusions from these. Through these he developed a new approach. He plunged wholeheartedly into reality and did not meet it with concepts as Newton had. Newton considered colors as a fan-shaped diffusion of light. This keeps all colors on an equal basis and they can only be distinguished quantitatively (by the number of vibrations per second). Goethe opened the path to a scientific, but not materialistic observation and treatment of color. His theory of color forms the essential basis of painting.

1.5 A journey through the color wheel: A concise theory of color for the teacher

The colors arranged in a wheel can be a source of inspiration for the painting lessons. The circle is created through two opposite forces, yellow and blue, which are united through intensification and mixing, representing the rising and falling processes, taking place in nature, calling forth the greatest possible range of colors. It is an inexhaustible source. When you pass your eye along all these different color qualities, images and experiences arises. They can evoke different times of day, different seasons. Randomness disappears and only the essence of things is expressed. One's own fantasy and ideas look after the rest and while painting you arrive at an understanding of the language of colors. As educators we must learn to speak this language, as fluently as possible to show the pupil the way in the painting process. This requires the educator to find new tasks and the correct order of the lessons.

The color circle is a world of its own. When you let this totality act upon you, you will soon be absorbed into a harmony. Goethe refers to this impression, which goes beyond the mere senses, as the sense-moral working of color, in this case colors working inside and opposite one another. Goethe himself, when viewing his organic color arrangement, said:

> Once you have really understood the opposite
> positions of yellow and blue, and have taken on the
> intensification to red, making the opposites come
> together and uniting itself to a third principle, the
> special thought will come to you, that these separate
> and opposite beings could have a spiritual significance.
> Then when you see how they create green below and
> red above, you can only think of, on the one hand,
> the earthly and on the other, the heavenly children of
> Elohim.

Describing the sense-moral workings of color, Goethe did not dare tackle until the end of his writings on the theory of color. He sensed he had discovered a special field. We can now take the step to enter the color circle, the color space. That which is called the third dimension in the physical space, creating a front and back, near and far, is not the perspective in this color space, but the expression of the qualities of colors. Red can come towards us. Blue moves away from us. The red warm pole goes through me, while the cool blue pole is endlessly far away. In this way I participate in the color circle. And when I go through this, I experience a great deal; soon I can no longer distinguish myself from the colors, I am living in it. The yellow-red always comes towards me and appeals to me, flows towards me radiating warmth and life. Blue pulls me along with it, gives me space and I can be myself. Presently we find ourselves between these opposite trends. This makes a clear impression on our souls. We move along with the changing impressions of colors.

We can try to describe these impressions gained when we "walk" through the color circle. Each color has several aspects, often positive as well as negative. In addition there are many nuances within the color itself. Through one's own experiences, in other words, through doing a list of characteristics, moods and properties can arise and be continually expanded and improved. Whoever carries this internally developing dictionary can draw richly from this for assignments. A condition is, however, that the entirety should remain in motion. For Goethe pointed out to us that these are processes. Taking part in a process oneself demands mobility, flexibility, and self-development and a conscious awareness of new experiences. Goethe's work is a base from which we can start. The experience of others can complement this. It is a matter of describing each color in the circle with a nuance of feeling. Some examples are:

White: The clearest shade of light. Peripheral and ever expanding. It breaks through barriers and is objective and cool. White quickly loses its purity.

Black: The darkest shade of light. Related to darkness. Searching for the center. Hermetically shut. It forms, limits itself. Pulls one inward into the depth.

Yellow: The color closest to the light. In its highest purity, yellow is clear, cheerful and brisk. It expands and enlivens the heart. It is a beaming color, which will not be restricted. Depending on its movement towards red or green, it exudes a jocular, teasing, reckless or quick witted mood. In a slightly impure state, yellow can have an unpleasant influence. It becomes a color of shame, evoking abhorrence and displeasure.

Orange: This color can enrapture us, even up to aggression. In addition it makes us strong. We feel strong. It gives us enthusiasm, joy and warmth. Orange is also festive. It entices us forth.

Red: Leads us into the middle of life, in the lively element. It can be solemn, splendid and bombastic. Strong and serious. Warm, proud, wrathful or angry.

Pink: Lighter shade of red. Mild and gracious. Memory of our eternal youth and our incarnation. Tender, soft and familiar.

Lilac: Tender, just as the color pink. It can however be coquettish and vain. Or, contrastingly, it can be serious. On its way to blue, it leads us to the inner depth of being.

Violet: On its way to red it can have quite a disturbing effect. It takes us along, forcefully.

Purple: It can also be lively, but then without cheerfulness. Modest and reserved towards a feeling of cosmic holiness in the blue-violet.

Blue: Not only quiet and enveloping, but also cold and chill. Closed off to the outside. Easily forms contours and silhouettes. It can emanate peace. Sometimes yields to us and creates space. Also has a receptive and calming mood.

Green: Green spreads peace and contentment. It has a harmonizing effect and is good for tranquillity. It can also be dull.

From our soul moods we search for colors that are suitable. Concretely we can paint a color circle and compose a series of moods: joy, sadness, shyness, slyness, thoughtfulness, and so forth. Where do these moods belong in the color circle? It can often be a balancing act. We need to explore whether a certain mood does or does not fit a certain color. In this way a soul moods color chart can gradually be built up, a color circle which becomes a focal point for painting lessons. In the first three classes, during which the children paint mainly soul moods, the teacher's preliminary work can be a good support. For example, in an animal fable a sly animal and a very courteously innocent animal meet. A meeting between two totally different soul moods. Which colors would one choose? Does the color from the cooler side of the spectrum meet a warmer color? Are we looking more for an introverted mood or one that's extrovert? Such considerations are necessary to arrive at a good dialogue of color.

Colors are important in their own right. The child will start to recognize the elements of the story and learn to distinguish between varying qualities. In doing so we arrive at a series of moods, characters and feelings, each having a place in the color circle: vain, mystical, coquettish, courteous, refined, philosophical, thoughtful, humble, introverted, receptive, pure, sad, detached, passive, calm, shy, timid, quiet, dull, certain, irked, sly, venomous, cunning, fresh, clever, happy, cheerful, buoyant, enthusiastic, beaming, pleased, surprised, elated, fanatical, active, pushy, incensed, angry, reckless, impetuous, overpowering, forceful, brave, proud, dignified, regal, and so forth.

Anyone will be able to find a person or an image from a story with a word from this series. The greater the number of adjectives (i.e., color nuances) in a story, the more living images and color riches are evoked in children. This is the basis for the teacher and pupil to develop an organ for the colors within and without us.

In a conversation with the painter Margarita Woloschin, Steiner says the following about the development of a lively concept of color in children:

> To the young child inner and outer world are only
> moderately separate from each other. With the outer
> impression the child also receives the quality of the
> individual color, something of its own character and

instinctively the child is still aware of the actual essence of red, of blue, of yellow and of other colors. This is lost as a child grows older. School children ultimately experience colors as properties of objects (the blue ball, the red roof, and so forth). This however causes the ability in the soul to be paralyzed, which impedes the further development of the soul's eye. Children often learn at an early stage that red and yellow are warm colors and green and blue cold, but in their experiences they can sense this less and less. In this way these judgments easily become an abstract and lifeless knowledge. If the true experience of colors is not nurtured in our time and the mechanical theories about the nature of color live on in humanity, children will be born on this earth no longer having an organ for the observation of colors.

That is why we in the Waldorf school work with the advice of Steiner to guide the children as early as possible through the world of colors.

1.6 Painting and the senses

The senses are the gateways to the world. They enable us to observe the world around us. Our senses develop throughout the different stages of our lives. Senses such as sight, hearing, and touch are generally well known. Steiner indicated new paths in the field of the senses. He subdivided everything that is available in sense impressions and experiences into twelve areas. They are clearly distinguishable, but at the same time inwardly related. You cannot actually describe one single sense without simultaneously knowing the others, so strongly are they interlinked. They form one composition: a unity formed by twelve senses. They can be split up into three groups of four, indicating the relationship of humans to the world in three layers: the will, feeling and thinking. Because the development of the senses is closely linked to the development of artistic abilities within people, a brief look at these twelve areas in relation to painting and color is appropriate.

The *sense of touch* we mainly experience with our skin, usually our fingers and hands. We constantly explore the world by touch. Is it hard, soft, rough, wet or dry? Everything gives a certain impression. These we perceive inwardly through our sense of touch. When exploring the type of paper, smoothing the brushes on the back of one's hand, dealing with the sponge, dampening the paper and dabbing it, our sense of touch is activated. This prepares us for working with colors. In this field there are plenty of experiences: wetting the paper and observing how the paper responds with regard to humidity, the cold or warm hands of the children, exploring the equipment. This is why it is best to let the young children do as much by themselves as they can.

With the *life sense* we observe the condition of our living body, particularly when it is unbalanced by fatigue, languor, hunger or thirst. Working with color evokes reactions in our living body. The child reacts to this with his life sense. With a proper variety of moods during the lessons, the life sense is stimulated: calm and quiet, activity and enthusiasm. An impediment to the development of the life sense is, for example, demanding too much from the pupils, including carrying on painting for too long or working too monotonously with a certain color.

The third is the *sense of movement*. Here we are not concerned with one's own ability to move. We are concerned with the perception of our own movements. This tells us whether our bodies are at rest or in motion. We can sense inwardly that we are moving. We do not need to look at our feet to know whether we move or stand still. Particularly in traditional children's games and folk dances, many movements occur which have a stimulating effect on the development of the sense of movement. Here we often come across rhythmic movements, alternating slow and fast sections. The sense of movement is constantly involved. The shapes that arise in a painting we explore with our eyes. The sense of movement causes this to happen. With the movement of our eyes we follow the contours. In the course of time we learn to describe these forms and movements that we perceive. From an educational point of view it is important to follow the brush (the painting hand) with the eye. When form-drawing this plays an even larger role.

With the *sense of balance* we firstly observe our own balance. In painting we are dealing with right and left, above and below, the diagonals. In the working of color and color perspective, we talk about before and behind spatial directions which we explore with our sense of balance. This results in an awareness of composition.

The above-mentioned four senses are distinctly inwardly directed. They primarily observe our own physical condition and are also called the physical senses. Through these four senses we are linked to our bodies. The young child in particular needs to develop these senses to be able to take the first steps into the world, literally and figuratively. Its stimulation is however also of great importance as a basis for intellectual and emotional development in the beginning of the primary school level, especially when gaps occurred during infancy.

The second group of four senses is related to the human soul, the feeling and perception world. They could be called the senses of the soul, their impressions always contrasted. When talking about the eye: something is beautiful or ugly; with the sense of warmth: warm or cold; with smell: pleasant or obnoxious; with taste: salty, sweet, bitter, sour. In connection with painting we pay attention not only to the *sense of sight* but also to the *sense of warmth* and the *sense of smell*. The fact that certain colors can evoke a smell or taste, for example earth colors, shows an intensive reaction evoking the perception of color in more, if not all, sense areas. Also the paints (particularly plant paints) and the damp paper and the neglected sponges are noticeable experiences during the painting lesson.

One of the most important senses with painting is the *sense of sight*. We can see immediately what we are doing: how the color area expands, how it relates to other colors. Color areas become images. We look and compare. The eye is a very active sense organ. More than three quarters of all impressions enter us via the sense of sight. When we have seen enough we "take things as seen." This is why it is important that the time in which the child is intensively busy is not too long. As the child grows up it can work more and longer, see and take in more. We all know the feeling we get when we overstay our visit to the museum. The first few paintings are observed the most intensely. We should take advantage of that moment during the painting lesson. The preparation should not take too long, so that the child can still observe the colors freshly.

The sense of sight is directly linked to the eye. "The eye owes its existence to the light. From no matter which animal organ the light calls forth an organ that becomes equal to itself and thus the shape itself to and from the light, so that the inner light can approach the outer light." (From *Goethe's Scientific Work*) Goethe also summarizes it poetically in the following way:

> Wär nicht das Auge sonnenhaft
> Wie könnten wir das Licht erblicken
> Lebt nicht in uns des Gottes eigene Kraft
> Wie könnt uns göttliches entzücken?

Translated this means: If the eye were not sun-like, how should we be able to see the light? If in us God's own power would not live, how should the godly be able to enrapture us? Goethe further explains: "That direct relationship between the light and the eye no one will deny, to think of both together as one and the same, is more difficult. In the eye dwells a calming light, which is awakened with the slightest provocation, internally or externally. We can evoke the clearest images in complete darkness. By daylight we can notice the least external influence of the light." With Goethe's remarks about the eye and the light we come to a greater understanding of other senses and realize how intensely we take in the outside world.

The blind Jacques Lusseyran uniquely pictures the inner observation of colors in his book *The World Begins Today:*

> The eyes create the colors. Not the physical eyes of course, the object of ophthalmology. The two tender organs positioned in the front of the head which are not the true reality are merely mirrors. Broken mirrors, but they keep on living. The essential eyes which I'm referring to function deep within us. Seeing is an extremely essential deed in life; seeing is an indestructibly strong act, independent of the physical instruments used for this purpose. For seeing derives from a life source, even before objects are seen, even before something presents itself outwardly in a certain form. One sees inwardly.
>
> If that inner light and consequently color (light's small change) had not first been given to you, we could not have admired the colors in the world. All this I know now, after twenty-five years of blindness.

Experiencing the *sense of warmth* or cold is only possible when our environment or the object has a different temperature from that of our own bodies; otherwise we feel nothing. The sense of touch would come to our aid in that case, but we won't know anything about the temperature. A good sense of warmth is of vital importance. Steiner calls this sense the first one. It is an elementary sense, present in all other senses. Our language has all sorts of expressions derived from our sense of temperature: "To warm up to something," "to leave someone out in the cold." The activity of painting and the general workings of color have a profound influence on the warmth organism of the child. The child experiences this. So we can say that the sense of warmth is also called upon in painting.

The third group, that of the higher four senses, is related to the sense of imagination. By means of these senses we direct ourselves more towards the outside world. We have to exert ourselves more for that which is outside of us. With the ear we know the expression "put one's ear to the ground." If we truly wish to meet someone, then we should leave our little house and go out to meet the other. In this group we include *the sense of hearing, the speech or sense of words, the sense of imagination* or *thinking sense,* and *the sense of "I."* The development of these senses is dependent on that of the so-called lower senses. In painting we address these senses in particular with the introduction and the review. The initial "looking" and "seeing" at best become "letting speak" and "hear" and consequently enjoying art and dealing with art.

When relating the development of the senses to painting, we can yet discover a distinction between the preschool and primary school child. In his last series of public lectures Steiner says that not until around the seventh year do the senses start becoming independent. From this time onwards the child can start an independent artistic process. With smaller children all sense impressions melt together into one whole impression. There is not yet a clear distinction between them.

The observations themselves do not yet enter into this consciousness. So we cannot yet speak of "observation, understanding and the merger into an image." The small child still gives himself up entirely to all the senses. Not until the child goes to school does the interest in usefulness, meaning or benefit of a certain impression come to the fore. The young child's thinking world is still bound to time and place. After the seventh year, elements from the past can be properly linked to the present. The free imaginative faculty will emerge, as will a growing sense of memory through which the child learns to produce a painting on paper. Visual impressions rather than aural often captivate children in primary school level.

The structure of the outside world also becomes more interesting to the children. They grab hold, as it were, with the forces they used for physical development before the seventh year. The ability to distinguish between light and dark for example, develops strongly, even doubles. Observing differences in color increases by ninety-percent from the seventh year. (Distinguishing pitch improves five-fold between the sixth and tenth years.)

So, from the sixth/seventh year, the child develops his own independent soul space in which to operate. Within this soul space the child paints. The younger child still, strictly speaking, paints from within. It is the task of the teacher to constantly enliven, address and further develop these senses. This helps to bring about a healthy respiration, circulation and digestion.

Well-developed senses enrich our lives. They are of vital importance. To them we owe a healthy attitude to the world around us. In the field of education, stimulating and activating the senses take up an important position. We try to open up these gates to the world for the children. At school, art education in particular contributes much to this.

1.7 Watercolor paints, painting techniques, equipment and materials

Watercolor paints

The soul element of the world expresses itself in the essence of color. Simultaneously color also gives expression to experiencing the human soul. Consciously or subconsciously we experience color in our souls. This applies to both our inner image or experience and our perception of what goes on outside of us. A sunny day puts people into a different mood than an overcast sombre day. On receiving bad news, we feel different from looking forward to a festive occasion. Thus on the one hand moods in nature are soul moods and on the other, the soul life can express itself in color. From the outside it is an impression; outwardly it is an expression. We are constantly dealing with the close link between color and soul moods. How can we best approach this lively relationship? The transparent medium of watercolor paint lends itself best for this purpose. It can unite both elements, color and motion. With this background in mind we predominantly opt for this type of paint and a lively, mobile technique, like wet-on-wet or "veiling." For the developing child watercolor paints are the ideal means for experiencing color and giving form. The child still has a great deal of creative imaginative forces and wants to use these. With color and water we can start to connect these creative forces with the fixed, crystallized world. In this the child learns to live. A bridge is built between what has already become and the creative power of the child. Time and again the children will experience, with each painting, the wet mobile paint which slowly dries up to fixed color forms or transitions. The process of becoming is the most important, in which the children can experience the working of color most intensely and give expression to their creative imagination.

The less condensed the painting, the more it approaches the essence of color. The purest form would be "painting with light." For example at sunrise and sunset. Also when there is a rainbow in which case we like to interrupt the lesson to let the children look at it. Just as nature keeps bringing out the colors in the atmosphere as if by magic, we experience the colorful lighting in a theater performance. The impressionists, in particular, picked up on this aspect. Color dances vividly in stripes, dots and areas across sky, water and landscape. Next to light and air (sometimes called the shade of light),[3] water is the next, more condensed medium to retain color and to make the color of light a manageable painting color. Water has a lively nature in its own right; it is pre-eminently the life-giver. Being transparent it is a good color bearer, ever ready to absorb color unselfishly.

Steiner describes how the creation of colors naturally relates to the water element. In earlier stages, during the development of the earth, the element of water came into existence through the workings of spiritual beings. Steiner referred to these as beings of the third hierarchy: archai, archangeloi and angeloi. The angeloi-beings become mediators, as it were, between light and darkness. From this activity colors arise. In the air and shadowlike darkness, all the colors of the rainbow begin to glisten.

Aristotle described in his brief scientific writings how the third hierarchy was involved in the creation of colors. This knowledge was lost in the course of the centuries. Because color spreads itself across the air-like element, the fluid, watery element comes into being. It can be compared to a process in which, under certain conditions, pressure causes counter pressure, "in the way, cosmically considered,

---

3. Steiner in *The Manifestations of Karma*, London: Rudolf Steiner Press, 1999.

the shade of light is air, so water is the reflection, thus creating color in the creation."[4]

We can recognize this element in the fresco painters, who painted on the damp limestone foundation. A still, peaceful water surface mirrors the interplay of color between heaven and earth. Landscape artists have been wont to find the water-rich areas because of this mirroring element. In particular, Turner's landscapes are not only examples of atmospherically color-rich paintings, but they show how to create a particular mood with optimal use of water, color, and light (i.e., paper). Cezanne's watercolors were a turning point in the history of painting. Opposite the nature image he set the counter image of the human spirit. In doing so he initiated a new phase in modern art. Subsequently we find the following words expressed by Klee: "Color has me ... I and color are one." Kandinsky's first image-free painting was a watercolor. This shining, lively painting represents the workings of and a renewed ambition to experience of color. Nolde, Kokoschka and many others followed.

Another new development was put into motion by Steiner, applied to the painting of the domes of the first Goetheanum. The painting foundation consisted of a mixture of paste-like white casein with wax, and balsam with paper cellulose. This was applied in several layers on cork sheets. All this was covered with a transparent layer. So Steiner eventually painted on a type of liquid paper layer. By doing this he developed a new kind of fresco technique, one free of form and restrictions. Steiner made large free floating color areas arise on these immense curved surfaces, images out of the color, moving, as it were, on the domes, with great color intensity. Special plant dyes were developed for this purpose by dissolving vegetable

4. See "The Hierarchy and the Rainbow," Dornach, January 1, 1924, from *Colour*, GA 291 [twelve lectures], London: Rudolf Steiner Press, 2001.

pigments in water, an intensive and time-consuming process at the time. Unfortunately none of this work remains because of the burning down of the building.

Vegetable dyes have only been manufactured and applied on a larger scale since the 1960s. The intensity of this type of paint is remarkable. The colors harmonize well. Their use in the classroom offers a special experience because watercolor allows the highest possible purity of color, and mixed with etheric oils it also becomes a boon to the nose.

Wet-on-wet technique

The term "wet-on-wet" is a little misleading. Here we are not talking about painting on such wet paper that colors would automatically run in all directions. "Liquid-on-liquid" would be a better term. After the paper has been moistened on both sides on a white painting board, it is dabbed with a sponge, so that a matt, moist shine becomes visible on the paper. Where it is still shiny, it needs to be drier; air bubbles disappear when the paper is carefully lifted and put back down evenly. In this way one can paint on a tight sheet of white paper. This enables the pupils to apply the colors in a transparent fashion, to expand the areas with ease and even to remove the paint off the sheet by means of a squeezed brush. Water around the paper should be removed with the sponge. When the painting is finished it should be placed slowly and evenly on a painting board to dry.

Veiling

Experiencing the "dissolving" and "drying up" is a frequent occurrence in the veiling technique, which allows for this technique in particular to provide many new valuable experiences. It builds on the experiences gained with the wet-on-wet painting. The veiling technique can be started in sixth grade. This is, of course, dependent on the existing skill of the class. The following are prerequisites: being able to distance oneself from the painting during painting, being able to understand the buildup of the colors, being able to handle the brush strokes and the fluidity of the paint to be applied. Many people automatically possess these skills. Color intensity and depth will give many a pupil the required carefulness in their work and the patience to let the layers dry in between times. A structural method is supplied with the curriculum for seventh grade.

First a paper type should be found which has a firm surface. The paper should be able to cope well with repeated wetting and drying without becoming "crumbly." It should also be able to absorb sufficient paint, otherwise painting will be over after three or four layers. On a watertight wooden or synthetic white board the paper is wetted on both sides. The paper should first be "worked out" (because it tends to expand, which you will notice when only wetting one side; the paper will then almost roll itself up, because the paper fibers expand on the wet side). Then the superfluous water is removed by dabbing with a sponge. Once the paper is smoothly and tightly on the board, all sides are fixed to the board with paper tape. During the drying process the paper stretches and is ready for the first veils.

Veiling can be done in various ways. In any case the following rule always applies: only paint in the same place once with the brush, otherwise the previously applied layers will be removed and dissolved whilst "brushing." The paint is thoroughly thinned so that initially the colors can be lightly applied. As more veils are painted, the paint can increase in strength, from initially very large to eventually smaller areas for the details. Just like wet-on-wet painting, it is good to expand the color from one area. In this case there is no need to know in advance how large the area should be or which form it will have eventually. As the paint on the brush runs out, let the area dissolve at the edges. Transitions between colors can then be made, without paying attention to the limits of the areas. The technique provides the pupil with a great deal of freedom, because all possibilities are left open and a form does not need to be rushed into so quickly. So, painting as dryly as possible, even though this may sound a little odd. Each wet spot will again require more patience in drying and can dissolve other layers. Another golden rule is: do not paint any areas which have the same shape, overlapping each other exactly. Rigid forms will then quickly arise and the mobility and possibility to remain within the process will become more difficult.

Veiling brings about an intensive color quality. The colors can be mixed and painted in all nuances. It is possible to "search" whilst painting and to arrive at shapes. Figures and images spring from the color areas. The work comes into being in time. Each day a little further. An important process for the pupils with new experiences, as it contrasts with the relatively quick work of the wet-on-wet technique. It provides the possibility to build up color qualities which are closely bound to the processes taking place in nature. While painting, one recreates nature, instead of copying nature in painting. This is an inner process, omitting the need to experience the outer. The results only become visible at the end of the process.

When carefully acquiring this technique, the pupils can meet the world of color in a renewed way. Those who want a result too quickly can have a nasty surprise, or yet arrive at quite an unexpected result, because veiling can be done to discover oneself, what things are about. This process is a perfect opportunity to get to know oneself; sometimes this will be torment, other times an unbelievably exciting event for those who dare take the challenge.

Paper, sponge and foundation color

Many types of paper are available and it is not easy to find the type appropriate for both wet-on-wet painting and veiling. In both cases the paper needs to be able to absorb a great deal of liquid. The surface must not break up or crumble too quickly. Apart from the quality of the paper, the cost also plays a part. Weekly painting with the class uses up a lot of materials. A thick type of newsprint provides good results and is affordable. Not pure white, but certainly suitable for wet-on-wet painting, available in 80 and 100 grams. Wetting just one side is often sufficient. A heavier paper type is needed for veiling. Preferably proper white. This is necessary for the working of the light through the various layers of paint. Always let the children feel the paper with their fingertips (watch out, the fingers should not be greasy).

With the more expensive types of paper there is a difference between the two sides. We always paint on the "roughest" side. The children can also feel the weight. Each paper type has its possibilities and limitations. Try it out as much as possible, the experiences in the classroom will provide an answer to which paper is the most suitable to which age-group. There is also the possibility to make one's own paper in a craft-lessons in third grade. This will give the children a different relationship to the material. This can be further explored in the higher classes.

It is recommended to wet the paper with a natural sponge. The different shapes and density provide an extra experience for the senses. The sponges easily absorb a great deal of water and not one sponge is the same as another. Synthetic sponges can also be used; they can be cut in two for the small children's hands.

Painting boards should be white as they can affect the working of the colors on the paper.

Paint and brush

Various types of watercolor paints are available on the market, including Stockmar, Talens, Winsor & Newton, and plant dyes, which are becoming more and more available. The choice once again depends on experience, quality and cost.

It is important to discover how the primary colors (yellow, blue and red) relate to each other, how the mixed colors are and whether it is possible to paint a harmonizing color circle out of the assortment of a certain brand. Through working with the paints, the vividness, lightness, strength and intensity come to the fore. Ultimately the choice depends on the teacher trying things out for him/herself, exchanging experiences and the pupils' reactions. It is important to prepare the watercolors a day in advance, so that, before the lesson, the paint can be stirred once more and poured into smaller jars. A small wooden plank with rounded indentations for the jars to fit in is very practical when handing them out and the risk of upsetting jars will be lessened.

Broad brushes of 18/20 mm are preferable. This encourages painting from the color area. Thin brushes stimulate drawing with colors. For the purpose of veiling even broader brushes can be used. The width also depends on the paper format. The hairs should be able to absorb lots of moisture and then in turn easily release it. Hairs that are too hard damage the paper and ones that are too soft give little grip. The brushes are best hung up with their hairs down. Telling the pupils about the origins of the wood, the hair and the casing of the brush will awaken their interest for those people who made them. Also, the teacher treating the equipment and materials with care and respect will contribute to a good work attitude and a mood suitable for painting.

2. Kindergarten and Elementary Grades

2.1 Handling the curriculum and the basic exercises for the teacher

The curriculum is like the waves on the sea. The argumentation and underlying thoughts, the humanitarian work that we also find in human biology run deep below the surface and blow like the wind through the air. They cause the wash of the waves. We re-encounter the reflection of these currents in the curriculum. This is why describing the curriculum is an adventurous undertaking, always involving a measure of restriction, because movement is indeed recognizable but it cannot be anchored or a curriculum quickly changes into a construct; by that I mean, "This is how you should do it." This is definitely the last thing we are trying to achieve. With the description below we have tried as much as possible to provide beacons to guide you in the right direction with direct references to human biology and the pupils' phases of development. This is why it is not enough for the pedagogue who works with children in the area of painting to derive various themes from the curriculum and to translate these into painting assignments. He also needs to understand the principles which work through the years. His insight into the working of color, springing from his own experience, is important for each lesson, as is his experience of the specifics required by art in painting.

For the pedagogue working with children up to the age of seven the development phase indicates treating painting as work and play from the imitation angle, without placing an emphasis on content. This arises from the story telling of the kindergarten teacher. Throughout primary school level there is a natural progression from experiencing colors in their own right to colors finding expression through images. After the interruption of working with black and white in ninth grade both currents of the creative process are in order at secondary level: color being able to express itself freely and giving expression to images and color.

The basis for working pedagogically in this way does not only lie in a clear and motivated curriculum, but also in the skill of the teachers themselves. For this reason, when the curriculum is discussed, a helping hand is given in the shape of basic exercises, in which experiences may be gained which are important for the artistic, that is to say creative, dealing with examples and guidelines for the curriculum. This makes the teacher run through the subject matter before this is done with the children in the classroom, because the curriculum is not fixed. It unfolds in the work of the individual teacher with his/her class.

At primary level, from first grade through eighth, not every teacher is an artistic painter. Painting is a talent, just as there are sculptors and musicians amongst teachers. Yet painting at primary school level is preferably done by the class teacher: the extra energy he/she invests in his/her own development has a decided pedagogical effect on the pupils. At secondary level, the subject teacher is introduced. There may be relative difficulty in developing pedagogy, because the teacher will have spent more time on his or her own artistic development. The personal nature and type of training were a consideration in setting up the basic exercises. The exercises for the secondary level teacher are specifically concerned with the reflection on the working of the technique or the theme in relation to the age-phase of the pupils.

Finally it should be stressed that a painting lesson is not a detached hour, but is linked by content and rhythm with other subjects and the daily and weekly program. The pedagogical value of that link comes into its own when the teacher–pupil relationship has been so embedded in trust and security that within that calm, space can be created to experience the finer nuances of color life and art life in general.

For the sake of curriculum readability, we have opted for texts without too many acknowledgments. Usually the source is mentioned directly with the quotes. The bibliography will give ample background reading, so that the interested reader can get his bearings clearly.[5]

2.2 Painting in the kindergarten

Play and imitation

In the Waldorf kindergarten the rhythmical element in the times of day, week and year play a major part. "Free play" in class has its fixed place in the morning each day, as does storytelling, singing and eating together. Usually after "play" other activities take place. Each day will have its own character. On Monday, for example, there will be drawing, on Tuesday clay modeling and so forth, always the same day each week. Everything is repeated in a set rhythm. This gives the children something to hold on to. They know where they

---

5. A chronological overview of Rudolf Steiner's quotes with regard to painting at school can be found in the book *Farben Erkenntnis* GA 291A, pp. 438–439. (The editor has not been able to find an English translation of this book.)

stand with a good daily and weekly buildup of alternate exertion and relaxation.

In this way painting is embedded in the weekly rhythm. Preschool aged children have a natural need to express themselves, to occupy themselves with color. They delight in the lighting up and darkening of colors. The children are surprised when new colors spring up on the paper. The objects around them have fixed colors, yet on the painting paper they move freely, they appear and disappear. Painting is therefore a great experience and the key to instinctively understanding how colors arise and change.

The preschool child imitating the adult is the pedagogical principle for painting in the preschool class. A painting "miss" is followed by the children. The children naturally wish to imitate the painting "miss" because they feel sympathetic towards her. Once she has prepared everything in the morning, she starts painting while the children enter the classroom. Even when taking off their coats, they can see their teacher at work. During the greeting she carries on painting as much as possible. Finally the children stand and watch her paint. They see each movement as it happens: handling the paints, water, brush and paper, the attention the teacher gives to the colors and how new colors arise on the paper or disappear suddenly just like that. It has a magic, fairy tale like quality.

This spurs the child's need to paint. "I would like to do some painting." "Me too!" The teacher interrupts her work and together they get everything ready. This is how they start working, imitating the teacher. It is important to leave the children the option to join in with the painting or to stand and watch. After all, working with colors requires a "force" really only released after the seventh year.[6] The

6. See Steiner's *The Education of the Child in the Light of Anthroposophy*, London: Rudolf Steiner Press, 1965.

soul of the young child sometimes has not enough space available to understand colors, which because of their different qualities, can evoke tensions, which the child resists. Just watching the interplay of color is sufficient for some children.

In the kindergarten class we do not speak of a painting "lesson." There are many other activities and the preschool child follows the work and play of the teacher in action, gesture and singing. The children can also be helpful in preparation: mixing and stirring the paint, filling the water jars, getting chairs and tables ready and so forth. The older children especially soon learn how everything should be made ready for painting. The teacher always sets the example.

It is also possible to invite an artist to create a painting among the children in the class, just like a bicycle repairman, blacksmith or baker can be at work in the class during work games. The children follow all the actions, the preparations and work approach of the painter with great interest. They will observe the artist's dedication and enthusiasm. "Yes, I want to be a painter just like him when I grow up," one of the children tells the teacher.

If a number of children show little interest in painting (and often do not follow the example in other activities) the teacher can think of a short story to try to encourage these children to join in. The content can be directly linked to everything involved in painting. Of course the most important fact is that these children at their age, do already have the faculties to occupy themselves with painting.[7]

---

7. Rudolf Steiner mentions in his booklet *The Education of the Child in Light of Anthroposophy* the two magic words, indicating how the young child connects with its environment. They are: imitation and example. He also describes how the Greek philosopher Aristotle called the human being the most imitative animal. For the child up to the change of teeth this statement is most appropriate.

What the children paint in kindergarten class should be left open. The three pure colors yellow, red and blue are at their disposal. (see also first and second basic exercises for the teacher) Assignments are not given. The color play on paper and in the water jar is a small adventure every time. Excitedly the children often give a commentary with their paintings. After school many a parent is pulled into the classroom by their child eager to show the outcome of his painting. It is not entirely dry yet and so gives a very lively impression. Never ask what it represents if the child does not give you an explanation itself. The doing, the experience is the most important aspect for the preschool child.

* Basic exercise #1 for the teacher

Which color do we use in painting in the kindergarten classes and the first grade? A yellow, a red and a blue. Out of these all other colors can arise. With which yellow, red or blue? If we start from what is available on the market, we have at least two yellow colors, two red and two blue: a lemon yellow and a golden yellow, a carmine red and a vermilion (cinnabar), an ultramarine blue and a Prussian blue. One of the two always stresses the cool, the other one the warm variant of the color. Lemon yellow tends towards blue and is a cooler yellow; it quickly becomes green. The golden yellow tends towards the orange/red, so is a warm yellow. So it is a matter of finding a middle, a neutral yellow. Both colors are needed to obtain the proper color. By mixing them, the teacher experimentally searches for a color that satisfies him/her. Searching and trying out for oneself will train the senses.

It is important to explore, observe, take distance when trying this out. Eventually one will have both a clear inner feeling for what is the proper red, yellow or blue and the skill to compose the colors quickly. This is an indispensable exercise for the teacher wanting to paint with young children. Later on, in the section on the second grade, the children will do this themselves. They will have at least the above six colors at their disposal. It is best to prepare the paints one day in advance of the painting lesson. The pigment will then be able to dissolve properly in the water.

This above process to find the proper yellow color is likewise necessary for the blue and the red. Ultramarine blue is a warm, reddish blue and Prussian blue is cool, ink-like. Carmine red is the deeper red and vermilion heads towards orange. Try to mix the pure red out of these. Do not be afraid of being a little beside the mark. The colors will be enthusiastically received if they are just that little bit different from usual.

* Basic exercise #2 for the teacher

After the three colors have been mixed with a little water, their compatibility should be considered. Do they form a harmonious whole together? How do these colors relate to each other? Does one dominate the other? How powerful is the yellow against the blue? In order to find out, it is a good idea to paint a small color circle. Yellow with blue gives a green. Blue with red gives a purple and red with yellow an orange. The circle is complete. Now observe the colors that have arisen. Watch the yellow against the purple, the green against the red, the blue against the orange. If we now consider the work in its totality, we can see whether the colors are balanced satisfactorily. Does the cool side dominate, does one color really burst out? Too much ultramarine in the blue can cause the blue to lump together. The pigment easily piles up. When this paint has been left standing for a day and not stirred before painting, you will see that the blue has sunk to the bottom with fairly clear water at the top. In this case it is difficult to make green and purple.

The Stockmar© brand has brought new colors not only under the name of "Farbenkreis Farben." From these colors a beautiful color circle can be painted. Unfortunately the red in particular shows a certain strong one-sidedness requiring a necessary adjustment in preparation.

Consequently the task for the teacher is to offer the proper colors to the children through exercise, colors which carry within them all possibilities. The right color is that which one finds best for a particular task, possibly producing individual differences.

2.3 Painting in the first grade
A journey of discovery through the land of color

The children have now taken the big step from kindergarten to the first grade. Now they are on their way through the twelve year curriculum. This also applies to painting. The colors have been discovered and explored in preschool and the names of the colors are known. Now every exercise will fit into a larger context. Step by step, region by region, the children discover the land of colors with all its rules and opportunities. The teacher draws the bowstring every year and the pupils experience dreamlike, with more or less consciousness, the objectives that the teacher is aiming for with his arrows.

For the first lesson, for the first school day, Steiner indicated a clear starting point. Using an exercise by and with the pupils, he points out directly the working of two different colors next to each other. In doing this he says to the children, "Now I want to tell you something that you will not quite understand yet, but which you will one day. It is this, what we have just done up there on our painting paper (placing yellow next to blue) is more beautiful than what we have done below it, where we painted green next to the yellow."

Let us take a closer look at these words. When looking for words to replace the word (for us sometimes loaded) beautiful, it soon becomes a lot clearer. Yellow, the first color to come into being when the light is obscured, and blue, the first lighting up in the darkness, are polar opposites. In a certain respect they are each other's extremes. Joined together they form green. This color green is consequently related to both and contains both. Goethe calls yellow/green and blue/green monotone color positions and yellow/blue characteristic. In this way Steiner agrees with Goethe when he used the words "more beautiful." If we look for other ways of describing both combinations (the children often come up with the best ones), we could include "more exciting," "more adventurous" or "more fascinating." The most important thing is that it is obvious that yellow and blue carry within themselves more opportunities for development than the other monotone combinations. Green/yellow and green/blue are more like brother and sister to each other. They easily flow into each other. These color tones are less exciting, less clear, and the colors light up less next to each other.

After all each mixed color obscures to a degree. So it always has less color strength. When intensifying the yellow and blue, even red is created (purple in Goethe's words). In this way light and darkness, active and passive, radiating and more introverted are the foundations of this first indication by Steiner. This is a first attempt at initiating a process within the children, not aimed at acquiring a fixed view, of what is beautiful and what is not in this world.

The second point to emphasize is the continuous use of two colors in painting using opposites. When form-drawing we find this in the curved and the straight and in music when experiencing an interval. Working from two different qualities summons alertness in the children. Painting exercises with one color, only red or blue, do not have this effect. Two different colors (or more) provide a healthy soul-tension—a feeling which stirs and stimulates the children. The first enthusiastic brush stroke leads to the next.

The six- and seven-year-old child can exchange the trusted imitative forces in this way for his own imagination and soul moving forces. He learns to move along from one color mood to another. Before the seventh year the child experiences the world in a more dream-like instinctive way. From first grade onwards we try to make the children more and more alert to the qualitative differences in colors. They recognize this from listening to fairy tales, for example. They sympathize with the prince, with the little girl in the dark woods or the mournful king deploring the loss of his daughter who is under a magic spell. Each mood is related to a color, and the teacher has to master this color dictionary. In this way each color exercise becomes a stage of development in the soul life of the growing child. The child learns to make his own decisions independently. Which color, where, and how?

In the painting lesson we do not connect the colors with the things surrounding us. For example, the sun is yellow—"As yellow as the sun." The blue of the sky. Grass is green. They are of course blatant truths, but in the first three classes they are not yet inspiration for the painting lesson. This is in contrast with therapeutic painting with children. In the lower classes we connect the colors to mood and quality, with adverbs, adjectives and verbs, not with nouns. Cheerful and happy, sad and afraid, enthusiastic and passionate, dull and unpleasant, stately and dignified, vain and regal. That is why we try to find basic moods in the images of the fairy tale. When you read a fairy tale you can always see the images before you in a certain color mood, as if you are wearing glasses that keep changing color. This link between image- and color-mood in the narrative subject matter is important for the teacher, a source of inspiration. For the children, however, it is not always important to know which fairy tale is at the basis of the painting lesson or from what the exercise stems. Without being aware of it they recognize the color mood of the painting exercise in their souls. A word not spoken exudes a force. The colors, the paint and the water, the paper and the brush offer enough to get started.

To stop the graphic or figurative from pushing aside the experience of the color mood, it is important to paint in large areas right from the start. This is why we use broad brushes.

The positioning of the color on the paper is left up to the children as much as possible. As far as mood is concerned, there is no right or left, below and above in the child's soul. Because the child at this age considers him/herself in the center of the world, he paints intuitively in and around the middle. It is however good for the teacher to know the other possibilities too. These often appear spontaneously on paper with the children when the movement of a color is emphasized. A movement is possible from top to bottom or vice versa, from right to left, left to right or diagonally across the paper. If the spontaneous division of the areas is uniform in the class and is repeated, other directions can be encouraged. It is fun to do something with this color movement on parents' evenings. Painting spontaneously from the center to the periphery will hardly occur then, as adults usually start on one of the edges. What remains important is that the teacher keeps on connecting with what the children have at their disposal by way of their own experiences. Freedom should be created where it is possible.

The totality of the color circle is constantly contained within the three primary colors. Offering these three colors in the lesson, yellow, red and blue, will provide us with all sorts of possibilities. For the teacher it is important to know which color tone combinations are possible. Although eventually the same color tone can come about, each new sequence of colors provides a new painting exercise. When red follows yellow, a warming element is added as it were: courage, nerve, strength. If red is there first and yellow follows, it lights up the color, clarifies, cheers up, makes everything more shiny. This applies then to all possible sequences. One color somehow always emphasizes the other.

This is what makes it exciting. Blue obscures the yellow to green. Yellow lights up the blue towards the same green. Yet two totally different experiences are at the foundation of this.

The color tones with two or three pure colors are: yellow/ red, red/blue, yellow/blue, blue/red, red/yellow, blue/yellow or yellow/red/blue, yellow/blue/red, red/yellow/blue, blue/ yellow/red, red/blue/yellow, blue/red/yellow. If we are painting with alternating large and small areas, the number of possibilities increases. A multitude of opportunities arises when involving mixed colors: orange, green and purple. An abundance of color conversations are possible for the first few years: color tones and color movements, soul movements, and soul moods.

Steiner pointed out how important it is to let the colors exchange places. If at one time yellow is in the middle and red is around it, the next time red can be in the center with yellow around it. These exercises have a very productive effect; they require a good degree of flexibility from the child's soul. Steiner expresses it this way, "In art education it is like this—the most differing things can be done in the most differing manners. It is not possible to say, that is definitely right or definitely wrong. We let the children express colors in such a way that they only paint from the elementary color imagination. One can say to them, for example, you have here in the middle of your sheet a yellow patch. Now paint a blue patch on a different sheet. Now finish it in such a way that all other colors change along with it." When the children have to change a color and focus on it totally, this makes a thorough interest in the color necessary.

Yet another aspect in first grade is the painting of the boundaries and unrestricted areas. Individual colors can be painted next to each other. A boundary is then clearly distinguishable between them. A boundary line arises where two color areas meet. Another possibility is letting one color flow into another. This creates a gradual transition, sometimes hardly noticeable, from one into the other. You paint the colors in such a way that you do not know where one color stops and the other one starts. The restricted form has a strong formative character. These forms arise from the intensity of the color itself. Red "forms" itself differently from yellow. Each color has its own form-expression. Children discover this in play when they exclaim, "Yellow feels pushed away into a small corner. Doesn't it want to shine?"

With the other possibility colors move towards and change each other. "The colors change each other as if by magic, see what wants to appear all of a sudden!" In order to describe these processes the teacher needs to have a series of suitable verbs, such as, magically changed, sweep along, overpower, give in, harmonize, and absorb. This is necessary preparation for the teacher's communication with the pupils. They, in turn, use these words to express what is happening on the paper. Closed and open painting should be done alternatively to prevent one-sidedness.

This takes us to the presentation of the exercise in class. During the painting lesson actual painting, not talk, is what it is all about. This sounds obvious, but consider it momentarily. An exciting fifteen-minute introduction which results in five minutes of painting, misses the mark. What is painting actually about? Many aspects have already been mentioned in the introductory chapters. It is about the moment the child connects, identifies, and plunges into the color. This happens from the moment the brush is dipped into the paint. Peace without distraction is necessary to achieve this. The child expresses herself, identifies with the color mood, an intense experience, and for many children quite exhausting after ten minutes or so. Working with color this way is the weekly soul nourishment for the child. A lesson two or more times a week is ideal. This colorful trip supports the child's development, even though the children only actually paint for a short time in proportion to the time needed for preparation, setting up and clearing away after the painting session.

The task can in that sense be offered in quite a businesslike manner. Often it will follow on directly from the previous lesson. The main thing is to make the painting task clear. Each teacher develops his/her own style to that effect. The teacher him/herself should be very clear about the mood, colors, size of paper, and composition. The teacher certainly does not have to involve the pupils in all this. Each situation, school, class, age, time of year, day, and so forth, also determines the class task. Too many words are unnecessary.

Before painting, the children's attention is brought to the outside, to the teacher's painting. In doing so he/she bypasses the speaking in the color world. We wish to achieve the complete opposite. The colors, supported by the spoken word, connect with the soul mood of the children. It is true, at this age, the children want to follow, imitate the teacher, but they themselves need to explore the new world of mood and color. Formulating the task limits and gives the pupil something onto which to hold. The children also understand the tasks largely from the logical buildup from the very beginning. In the higher classes a colored chalk sketch, some areas, lines or words can sometimes be necessary.

The skillful aspect of painting can be shown now and again, possibly accompanied by songs or poems. Each teacher can let his / her imagination go. It often needs to be pointed out how the brush should lie freely within the hand. The children could stroke the hairs of the brush again on the backs of their hands to feel a difference between soft and hard. When pressing the brush hard and straight on the paper, things will be damaged. Paper soaked in water is vulnerable.

The brush stroke should not be too rushed either. No big strokes next to each other. "We're not sweeping the floor or painting doors." In the first few years especially, it is exciting to discover the degree of dry or wetness for painting without the paint running on the paper and the child watching (as a spectator) what the colors are doing to each other. The other extreme is painting too dry, where the colors get stuck, so that movement is completely out of the question.

Steiner put it succinctly, "An inner sense of color build up should be developed in the children so that they acquire a feeling for the color world in experiencing fairy tales. When they let the imagination work, shapes will also arise, letting the forms grow out of the color. You can speak with the children in the color world."[8]

Summarizing we can say that there are at least three possible ways to arrive at a painting task: colors speak together and a color story arises; an image coupled to a fairy tale can be translated into a color mood; a color tone is painted as an exercise without involving the narrative element.

If we hang up the works with care and insight the children's eye will be trained. One of the possibilities is hang the paintings with the softer color tones at the top and the paintings with the more

8. See Rudolf Steiner's *Conferences with Teachers,* November 15, 1920, Forest Row, England: Steiner School Fellowship, 1989.

powerful colors at the bottom. Combine this with the paintings that show weak color forms (on the left, for example) and contrast those of strong color forms on the right. For reviewing the work refer to Chapter 4.1.

* Basic exercise #3 for the teacher

Paint a large scale color circle. Try to let as many colors as possible come about, a large variety of mixed colors. Now, while watching a small section of this color circle, try to find out, to experience, which mood this color expresses. Write down the color mood on the outside of the color circle. Eventually you will have an edge full of words. Sometimes certain soul qualities lie very closely together. Green can be sly, calming, dull, depending on its place in relation to the yellow and blue. In this exercise we are not concerned with pinning down the colors onto a certain mood in a fixed and dogmatic way, but rather to exercise one's own mobility of soul—to be able to put these into words, to move along in the color circle. Perhaps the following day different words will surface. Being involved is most important and always forms the basis for the tasks, especially for second and third grades where the soul moods are more and more profiled. This color circle is very apt for the narratives (stories). The color circle is like a living thing, in which colors are born and change, a feeding ground for the development of the young child's soul.

2.4 Painting in the second grade

Complementary colors – Color mood and color movement

The first grade pupil feels at home in the world of color and is quite conversant with the initial painting skills. Yet it still remains important for the time being to correct the posture in painting and in the care and use of the equipment. Standing while painting, which can also be done in the first year, offers the pupil a little more distance from the work and gives the child more freedom of movement. It can however create unrest. In this case it should always be considered what is more important; the quiet and calm in the work attitude or potential stumbling and movement while standing. The children have their own preference in this respect. The most important thing is that each child has a loose relaxed work posture, rather than a cramped style.

We continue with the idea of soul moods in second grade. With the new narrative subject matter the moods are more closely and more extensively described, also by the pupils themselves. The narrative subject matter contains a wonderful polarity. On the one side fables are told, on the other legends about saints. In the fables the (specific) characteristics are described in a short and powerful fashion. The animals have short adventures. Often two opposite "types" meet—wolf and sheep, bear and fox, fox and raven, and so forth. The differences then are most pronounced. Each animal thinks, speaks and acts from its own nature. Thus the sly and the naïve meet, the silly and the clever, the industrious and the lazy. From the theory of color we would call these contrasts "complementary." Goethe calls these strongly contrasting combinations "harmonious." Red-green, blue-orange, and purple-yellow. In each combination the three primary colors are represented, blue opposite yellow/red, and so forth. We often find these opposites in the legends of the saints. A human, confronted in all sorts of special situations by his less good or animal characteristics, tries to overcome these by means of an inner path. Where hunger starts gnawing, a person decides to go on a fast. Francis of Assisi calls his own body "brother donkey." He tries to distance himself from his physical self in order to come to grips with it. He imposes his own will on it, underpinned and inspired by a great ideal and belief. The images of fables and legends are offered to the children. The painting lesson links up with this. Conscious use of "pure" colors adjacent to mixed colors should be encouraged in such a way that harmony and balance are achieved. "How large and powerful should we paint the peaceful green when it meets the powerful fiery red, without one lording it over the other?" Time and time again it is obvious that the active colors should be withdrawn in quantity to give the other a good chance, to let it be equal.

With the mixed colors we always have a choice between two paths, for example, the purple from the blue and then red or the other way around. Equally there is no need for one color to be always in the center with the other around it. All compositions are possible; the children can choose for themselves. Boundaries which arise strongly between the colors can be different (meandering, angular).

If a child happens to have his birthday on painting day, the following exercise is a possibility: yellow is in the middle, it is cheerfully beaming. Today is its birthday party. Red and blue are coming to visit and together they offer yellow the purple. Now the yellow is beaming even more with happiness because the much darker purple lets the yellow light up wonderfully. This is how the complementary colors influence each other. Red becomes even redder next to the green, orange more fiery next to the blue.

We now take a look at the legends. These give many points of contact for a color conversation with the children. The children hear how Francis, with one single gesture tames the ferocious wolf, who had been making the town of Gubbio unsafe for a long time—tames him and leads him back into town like a meek lamb. To prevent the children from painting a representation of this meeting instead of a color conversation, it is recommended that these painting exercises be done a few months after the story is told. The teacher as well as the pupils have to build up the story again bit by bit to be able to visualize the motif again clearly. With an introduction by the teacher, such as, "We are now going to paint this and that and you remember I am sure, because I only just recently told you the story." The children are too quickly left to their own devices or pay too much attention to externals. This is not recommended.

In the Francis story the first meeting with the animal is the most important motif. The teacher can try to find such characteristic meetings in the large number of stories available. They are extremely suitable for painting assignments. They are a clear topic of conversation for the children. What did Francis feel when he suddenly met the wolf? And what about the wolf? Did he give up immediately? Let everything the children have to offer be considered as much as possible. If we want to paint this meeting, which colors should we choose? Which would you choose for Francis, and what about you? Why? Good, you take that color later and you try out your color. And now the wolf. Who has thought of a color for the wolf?" This is how the class makes the colors appear as if by magic. Each child makes a choice and, surprisingly enough, the majority opt for the same combination. Yet different choices are the icing on the cake. After all, when the paintings hang up in class the next day this encourages more discussion. When the children are used to painting from the color area and from the mood, no naturalistic wolves and Francis figures will appear on the paper. From the color area and the quality of the color different forms appear. The *color movement* comes forward. The color, chosen for Francis, moves towards the other "wolf color." What is the response of that color? Does it give way or will it come to the front strongly? The paintings provide the answers. They are like windows into the children's soul where this marvelous meeting takes place.

In the course of second grade we can, in order to expand the possibilities, replace the three primary colors offered so far with two each yellow, blue, and red colors. On the market are lemon yellow and golden yellow, vermilion red and carmine red, ultramarine blue and Prussian blue. This supplement is necessary to obtain a rich nuance of mixed colors. The fresh green arises from mixing lemon yellow with Prussian blue. Ultramarine blue (containing a great deal of red) gives a beautiful purple together with carmine red. Vermilion red with golden yellow gives a warm and festive orange. In this way the children discover rich color nuances in the process. The children should have the feeling that the world of color is an endlessly large world and is not meticulously limited by what is available from the teacher.

We know a short example by Steiner in which many aspects of a second grade painting exercise are covered. You can speak with the children in the world of color. Over there is the coquettish lilac and a cheeky little red is on its neck (close to it or on the skin). The whole stands on a humble blue.

Where is lilac in the color circle if it should be a coquettish lilac? Is coquettish lilac large or small, and where is the red? How large is a cheeky little red actually? All questions aimed at the position of colors in relation to the other colors in the color circle. Questions about the possible composition, about size and position. Many facets are brought up in talks with the children and each painting will come out differently each time. Steiner indicated that these exercises could be executed fifty-fold. This gives the teacher, on offering, and the children, on working it out, a great deal of room to move, a space which has come about through a color conversation and not by letting the children sort it out for themselves. This would cause the work to lose its great pedagogical value.

Thus the feeling for color is further developed in the second grade. The color characteristics are reinforced. Through the contrasts in word and image, and actually painting, the eye and the heart are trained. The young child is allowed to experience each step as a new discovery and the teacher gives the space to use these newly acquired skills. In summary, with regard to the build up of color exercises in the first three classes, we can say:

> First grade: the notion of color and subsequent exercises
> Second grade: gesture and movement
> Third grade: forms and figures

* Basic exercise #4 for the teacher

The paintings which are discussed now refer to three examples Steiner provided in the first lecture for artists.[9] We start from a green color on the painting paper and place a red color in it. Two or three red areas are surrounded by the green. We do the same on a second sheet with blue. A blue/green color tone springs up. Then a third time with a soft pink, called peach blossom by Steiner. Three different colors exist within the green. These evoke three different reactions. It requires some skill in its own right to paint the color areas with good boundaries near the green. The green is best painted by mixing lemon yellow and Prussian blue. In fact here we are painting a complementary color (green/red), a monotone color (blue/green), and a color which harmonizes well with the green, peach blossom. Steiner summarizes the various impressions thus, "Imagine you would see this: Across a green field red people are walking, or across a green field peach blossom colored people are walking, or even blue people are walking across that field. In all three cases a

9. See Steiner's *Farben Erkenntnis*, GA 291A, not translated.

completely different range of experiences. On seeing the first scene, you will say, those red people I see in the green, in the green field, they bring that entire green field to life. That field becomes even greener by having red people walking in it. The green becomes even more saturated, even livelier, because of those red people. And when I watch these red people the way they just stand there, it makes me furious. Then I say, actually it is senseless, it cannot be this way. I should really paint these red people like flashes of lightning, they should be moving. Because quiet red figures in a green field cause tension because of their peace—they are already moving due to their red color, they cause something in that field which actually cannot possibly remain at peace. So out of necessity I end with a complex experience if I really wish to establish such an idea." Let us stop the lecture here for a minute. The trend described above is typical of a complementary color notion. The exercise can now be repeated from this observation and description, but now in such a way that the red truly acts in lightning-like figures, containing the quality red has in relation to green.

We continue with Steiner's description of the color of peach blossom on the green. "This is quite possible. People like these, with their peach blossom color, can stay there quite peacefully, even if they stand there for hours, it won't bother me. My feeling tells me that these peach blossom colored people do not actually have a special relationship with that field, they do not cause any tension in that field, they do not make it greener than it already is, they are completely neutral in relation to this field. They could stand wherever they please, they do not bother me there. They fit in anywhere. They have no inner bond with the green field." The exercise for the teacher from this example is as follows: Paint the peach blossom areas in round, curved forms and find within this the greatest possible peace and harmony in relation to the surroundings. This color impresses itself upon the green.

"I am now going to the third example; I am watching those blue people in that green field. What, you see, cannot even hold out, not endure at all. Because the blue in the green suppresses the entire green field. The green of that field becomes dull. That field does not stay green at all. Let us try to imagine: In a green field blue people or whatever creatures they are, are wandering about—they could be blue spirits haunting the field—just try to picture it. The field then ceases to be green, it even takes on a bluish hue. And if those blue people were to remain long on that green, it would all slip away from me. Then I would find myself thinking that the blue people are trying to carry off the field and dispose of it in some deep abyss. A green field cannot stay as it is if there are blue people in it, they take it up and make off with it. This is how one can experience color. And we must be able to have color experience or we cannot grasp what the world of color is at all. The imagination is a fine and beautiful instrument but we must experiment with it if we want to discover this for ourselves." From this discussion it is obvious that the blue absorbs the green as it were; as if the green is drawn away into a deep hole. In our exercise we can now paint the blue in such a way that the blue drags the green into the deep. [The paragraph above draws mainly from John Salter and Pauline Weille.] These exercises lead us to the workings of color. In class assignments we come across a multitude of possibilities in this area.

We should ask ourselves each time, how does the color work and which form, which trend, which gesture is expressed? These experiences link directly with the painting tasks of second and third grades.

2.5 Painting in the third grade

Drama in color experience

The pupils in the third grade complete a particular phase in the painting lessons, a phase in which the color, as a soul mood, sets the prevailing tone. The subject matter, the Old Testament, offers the possibility to give a certain dramatic climax to the soul moods. In the series of events from the stories, tragedy and joy of living play alternating parts: the creation of the earth, the deluge and Noah's Ark, Joseph down the well and his high function in the Egyptian court, the long adventurous journey of the Jewish people under the inspirational leadership of Moses, the young David beating Goliath—plenty of passages full of images to inspire the painting lessons and to arrive at colorful paintings, without falling into representation ("head" work). The drama in the color world takes place in the feeling world of the child. Remarks such as "it doesn't really look like … " can be avoided by emphasizing the color content of the work, together with character and gesture.

The line started in first grade continues: drama in the color compositions, in contrasting color qualities, in color transitions and delicate color nuances or in harsh color area boundaries. The children control the elements: limiting the color area and the flowing together of colors. They now also have the necessary skill to handle water, paint, paper and brush. They have it all "at their fingertips."

Color circles, where colors flow into each other, or, contrastingly, where they stand strongly adjacent to each other, are favorite subjects. It becomes more exciting when part of the color circle is restricted and the other colors are painted in an unrestricted way. In this way the areas can move through the color circle by a series of exercises. Each time a new effect arises from the color circle. The children discover how important the restricted areas are in relation to the colors flowing into each other, the fixed against the fluid, the waking element as opposed to the sleeping. Each color will acquire its own form and gesture, and together they continue to form a whole. This is still completely appropriate to the development of the third grade pupil. The world is still experienced as a unity, even if not for much longer. The eight- or nine- year-old child still joins easily with what is happening in the class. There is no critical stance. He sees the teacher as an authoritative element, a master, who leads the group in the activities throughout the school day. Organization should not be a problem any longer.

The Creation stories are a rewarding subject for the painting lesson. Each new day of the first week of the creation brings new elements. The children still pick these out from the moods, gesture, and movements a color carries within it. Yellow directs itself more to the periphery, always from a center point. Blue directs itself inward, feeling its way to a center. It can be submerged within itself. Red moves within itself, outwardly as well as inwardly. The mixed colors are nuances of these three movements. The separation of earth, water, air and fire does not need to be painted yet in a naturalistic way. This would not appeal to the child's soul as yet. The impulse for this will come from fourth grade onwards. In third grade we can search within the colors themselves to represent the Creation. Which colors tend towards fixed form? Which ones love to be tenuous and thin, to portray air and water? In principle all colors can be considered in this way. Blue can be applied lightly/airily and a yellow can have a fixed, limited, heavy form. The children can find these colors for themselves. They create their own world in doing this.

Now follows another direction for the teacher. A Creation day painting can have light carmine red as its basis; that is, the entire sheet of paper is painted a light red. A warm, expectant glow is a good basis for the ensuing work. It helps to bind the other colors. Surprisingly enough, the "foundation" is not such a determining factor in the end result, as one would expect. It disappears to the eye, yet it still retains its effect. When we read about the initial phases of the development of our earth in Steiner, we discover that the first described lessons was a condition of warmth weaving within itself, an inner warmth as a basis for all further development.[10] Painting a foundation opens up many new picturesque possibilities. A yellow or blue undertone for a painting brings about an essential change. The children themselves will start to discover the various effects these undertones have. There is yet another advantage. As a start to a painting lesson painting an undertone creates a great deal of calm in the class. Almost in a carefree way the children can create the right mood on the paper. For the teacher it creates the opportunity to observe the way the children handle the brush. Children tend to go "through" the paper instead of stay on it. The idea is to create from color, not to create "something." After all, the Creation of the third day, for example, was more than a simple landscape, complete with horizon. We would be doing an injustice to the image that we have painted so richly with words. One should prepare the formulation of the assignment well, to leave enough unsaid, so that the image remains full.

Depending on the pupils, we should be able to paint figures in the second half of third grade. From color quality and movement it is in fact a small step to create a figure, a human figure. It could however also be a trap for both class and teacher when the representative element is too strongly emphasized. Silhouette-like figures arise on the paper, which can nullify the many skills and artistic processes

10. See Steiner's *The Evolution of the Earth and Man*, New York: Anthroposophic Press, 1987.

which we have built up so far. Painting little puppets is not the intention. The inspiration from the great images of the Old Testament can help the teacher and the children as soul preparation for starting up an artistic, colorful process.

A measure of caution is required to enable soul movement, painted in words, to become soul movement which takes on color. The figure will then automatically appear. This does not need to be a human figure. Details on the face, arms and legs are not under discussion as yet. Color movement evolves and this expresses the soul mood of the character from, for example, the Old Testament. Wrath, joy, doubt and sadness often come up in the stories. Sleeping, dreaming and waking could also be motifs from which to work. Yellow, blue and red can, from their mood and movement, become a Christmas mood, a theme that can be used in all classes.

The story of "Joseph thrown down the well by his brothers" could be a good introduction as a figure motif. How does Joseph feel? Which color best expresses his mood? Once this fundamental color mood is established, the entire sheet can be covered softly. On top of this we paint the figure in the same color, in one area, making an inward gesture, lightly inclined towards a sad mood. A monotone mood arises. This could be blue on blue. Choosing the same color for figure and surroundings has the advantage of not making the figure jump up from the whole; it is taken up in the whole. The figure's contours do not contrast so strongly against its surroundings. Failed attempts are also avoided. After painting the figure, the children can then, in their own way, strengthen the surroundings. Choosing blue for "Joseph down the well," they could tend towards purple-like with red or green-like with yellow. Below the figure some darker painting can be done so as not to let the figure float, but to give it something onto which to hold. We distinguish three stages in this way:

1. determine color mood for the foundation
2. paint color movement
3. adjust surroundings

Joseph's sombre mood "down the well" is very different from the happy and beaming mood in the painting of Joseph as viceroy. The colors speak for themselves. Another example is Moses coming down the mountain with the ten commandments and seeing the people worshipping a golden calf. "Moses is not angry, no, we speak of the wrath of Moses. Children, what color is the wrath of Moses? What movement does this color make or what does that color want?" The conversation is set into motion and the children choose the colors.

The task for the children becomes more difficult if we choose a color for the figure which is adjacent in the color circle to the one chosen for the basic mood. For example, a purple figure in red or blue surroundings or a golden yellow figure in green or orange-like surroundings. Depending on the class potential, combinations can be made which Goethe calls characteristic colors: yellow with blue, red with yellow. Green with purple the children will find risky, but why not? Can we make figures appear from all these color tones, people from the Old Testament or, possibly figures from one of the yearly festivals? Painting several figures together with the complementary colors are assignments which will be covered in fourth and fifth grades. Good observation and a proper insight into the class limitations set the pace. All assignments based on the human figure from Aaron to Zeus (fifth grade) stretch over several years of learning and can be covered in lessons-slots. It is very important to make sure that the figures do not become stencil-like *on* a background but stay color movements *in* a surrounding. The color should not burst, as it were, from the paper like a cut-out silhouette; this would become a fixed image in the feeling life of the child. Rather, the whole, the harmony within a painting, should be borne in mind constantly. By alternating the assignments, by letting the pupils repeat the exercises "differently" and by reviewing them together afterwards, their observation is trained and the soul processes are started up and addressed.[11]

* *Basic exercise #5 for the teacher*

This exercise helps in exploring the six colors: lemon yellow, golden yellow, carmine red, vermilion red, ultramarine blue and Prussian blue. Paint a yellow color on a well-prepared damp sheet. This color covers the entire sheet. Now we should involve as many color nuances as possible within the yellow, so that the mood remains yellow, even though the color finds itself in the border areas of green or red/orange. On the one side the yellow tends towards the green-like yellow and on the other side towards orange. In an intensive scrutiny of the sheet more and more varying tints of yellow can be discovered. This exercise can now be repeated with red as the central color, tending towards purple and orange on the edges. To this purpose we can paint golden yellow and vermilion and on the other side Prussian blue and/or ultramarine blue. With the third exercise using blue, the green-like and red-like will appear. Repeat this exercise also with the mixed colors orange, green and purple.

Finally we can lay these six paintings in a circle. A magnificent color circle appears. This exercise can also be done as a group exercise on parent evenings. Each parent chooses a color and explores the boundaries of the chosen color. The outcome always surprises the parents and the experiences gained from a certain color can be exchanged.

---

11. See didactical directions in Chapter 4.

★ Basic exercise #6 for the teacher

The sixth basic exercise which we would like to include is the two-fold example Steiner provided in a lecture held in Oxford on August 22, 1922.[12] First, we need to create the right context. The lecture concerns the long-term teacher–pupil relationship and how the artistic pedagogical process via the temperament and the nature (more directed towards head—or more towards metabolism / limbs) will lead to the child's individuality.

With a subject like painting this could mean, for example, that the teacher will not let all the children paint the same thing, but that one child is encouraged to center the colors from the yellow-lilac and place them next to each other mixed. Here we are dealing with the child in whom the impressions "remain stuck in the head."

An alternative assignment gives the other approach to the child where all impressions flow away directly from the head into the remaining organism, as it were. The colors are more mixed in this case and the drawing-like element is used in the brush strokes; from the center between violet and yellow, it is as if the violet flows away, dissolves or fans out upwardly. The color fades, the line becomes important. Watercolor is, according to Steiner, the medium in which this exercise should be set. He continues with the example of how these two differently natured children should be approached in the physical education lesson with tasks that transgress the subjects. He not only pleads for the work of the class teacher who gives all subjects so that the teacher can be optimally involved in an artistic pedagogical process, but he also gives an example of how the task becomes an individual one. Each child should do it independently. "A closed form arises which starts to shine within itself." Also

12. Steiner, Rudolf. *The Spiritual Ground of Education*, New York: Steiner Books, 2003.

characterized as "becoming melancholy in the head." The fanning out shape is used in the flowing away of what has been learned from the head "like a sieve." Movement and line are emphasized more in the action of the child. In this way we connect pedagogy with what the child is and inventively give this color, form and direction on the basis of our observations of the child during the other lessons.

Here follows the translation of Steiner's words in the Oxford series. So the first exercise can be started from yellow-blue-red (violet lilac) while the colors remain adjacent to each other. In the second painting we use yellow-blue-red again next to each other and subsequently we let the blue-violet fan out upwards with long brush strokes. Likewise with the red.

It concerns the contact between teacher and child veritably being immersed in an artistic element. This will often cause the teacher to know intuitively, instinctively, how he should deal in relation to the individual child at a given moment. Let us, in order to clarify this, imagine the matter as concretely as possible.

Imagine, we have a child before us with learning difficulties. We notice: The images we offer, the feelings we wish to awaken, the ideas we wish to give the child—all this produces such a strong blood circulation and such a nerve impulse in the head, that the thing I want to impart to the child cannot, as it were, penetrate from the head into its remaining organism. The physical organization of the head becomes partially melancholic in a manner of speaking. The child has difficulty sending on messages from perceived images or what she experiences. What has been learned somehow gets trapped in the head. It can not permeate the rest of the organism.

Specifically all artistic elements in upbringing and education will be entirely instinctively tuned to this, when guiding such a child with an artistic feeling. To a child such as this I will impart the painting, working with color, entirely differently from other children. And it is important to point out that this is why painting has been part of the Waldorf education from the outset. After all, I have told you how writing is developed from painting. In painting we can approach each child individually, because the child has to do everything herself.

Imagine I have a child before me, the way I have just described her. I let her paint. Then, if there is a proper artistic contact between teacher and pupil, something will appear on that sheet of paper the child is filling with color that is completely different from another child.

Let me show you roughly, schematically, what should appear on the paper of such a child, where the impressions, the ideas get more or less stuck in the head. More or less the following should appear [see drawing below].

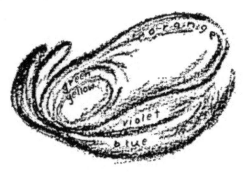

A color patch (yellow) will appear, then this type of color patch (lilac) because it is about the harmony of the colors. Then there will be here a transition area (orange) which will stretch a little further and the whole will be closed off on the outside (blue). This is how the sheet will look with a child whose ideas remain stuck in the head, as it were.

Imagine now, I have another child, where the ideas do not at all remain stuck in the head, but leak through it as it were, like through a sieve. Everything sags into the body, the child cannot hold anything because his head is a sieve. There are holes in it, everything seeps through. You should be able to experience that the condition of this child is such that the circulatory system wants to absorb everything from the rest of the body.

Then you instinctively, intuitively want this child to follow directions and cause something entirely different to appear. With such a child you are likely to see the following appear on paper [see second drawing]. You will see that the colors take on less closed off, less rounded shapes. You will see them elongate more and the painting turn into drawing, with loops appearing that take on more of the character of drawing. You will also notice that the colors are not so differentiated: In the first drawing they are strongly differentiated, but here [see the second drawing below] they are to a lesser degree.

When we paint with proper colors—not with that awkward chalk, which does not allow one to show this properly—we will be able to have a curative and healing effect on those properties of the children we have discussed; on the one hand through pure color, on the other colorful forms.

There is not a direct indication as to the age, but in view of the other subjects discussed in this lecture and considering the skills necessary to execute this exercise "technically," we estimate the age to be that of the second to fourth grade pupil. Whether and how often the exercises can be repeated is not mentioned and therefore dependent on the insight of the pedagogue who knows the children. Such pedagogical and therapeutic directions by Steiner do not occur often in the area of painting. This is why it is important for the teacher to know this and gain experience with it in order to make new discoveries him/herself.

2.6 Painting in the fourth grade
From soul- to nature-mood

From the ninth/tenth year of age the child acquires a new relationship to the world around him. He is starting to become more aware of the home and school environments. The look in the eyes changes. The open, expectant look becomes more of a questioning, sometimes judging and critical look. Children this age become self-critical. They become embarrassed by their own painting and drawing work. "It's gone wrong, it does not look like it should at all." The others are not spared either. Parents, teacher, fellow pupils all of a sudden have to take the rap. For example, they make comments about clothing, hair, that funny nose or big ears. Everything is different from before. The child is full of insecurities. The former automatic flow of sympathy for the adults has disappeared. The eyes have been opened. And not everyone in the child's surroundings finds this a pleasant experience. Experiencing death sometimes comes very close. The child can start to feel lonely. Insecurities can be camouflaged by provocative behavior, a big mouth and the need to look tough. "How this child has changed in the last few months!"

the teacher sighs to a colleague. Parents bring up the sudden anxiety of the child. "She doesn't dare be alone in the house and the light has to stay on all night." Everyone is bound to remember this from their own childhood.

The new relationship to the world also has a flip side. For example, the children can make surprising discoveries in nature. The things that were so taken for granted before are now discovered as something new. Interest in the environment has been aroused and the curriculum responds to this with, for example, human and animal biology and geography. By means of these the children discover that images and forms, which up to now they had experienced inwardly, can be found in the realm of nature. The teacher, in the style of Goethe, tries to let the children practice the phenomena of the manifested world and recognize those forces at work in nature. Everything which was practiced up to the fourth class with regards to soul moods now needs to undergo a metamorphosis, a change: from soul mood to nature mood. The glance/perspective is directed outwardly. The animal world is especially close to the child's world: the animals in the field, on and in the water, the birds in the sky, animals in the different elements. They shape, feed and color themselves in accordance with their environment. The great relationship between people and animals becomes obvious in the human- and animal-biology lessons. We avoid a lifeless naturalistic view in this, so that nine- and ten-year-old children learn to build a bridge between the earthly manifestation (image) and the creative forces within it.

Earth colors, mythology and the landscape

When painting nature moods, landscapes and animals, children feel the need to paint "darker" colors than the primary colors red, yellow and blue, and the mixed colors orange, green and purple. Colors mixed of the latter group have already naturally and spontaneously appeared on the painting paper: the brown and grey-like colors. These colors are particularly exciting to paint with, even though a number of children will find it difficult to produce pure and clear color tones. It is as if a shadow is cast on the sheet. Being able to enjoy this new color quality hangs together with the child's discernment. Where one child can only see "dirty brown colors," another child discovers many interesting color nuances on the same sheet.

The color exercises, as given in the sixth basic exercise for the teacher, are still too difficult for this age group. Part of it, however, is possible, for example a color exercise with primary colors in which a mixed color arises (e.g., orange), which is subsequently lightly painted over with the complementary color (blue). In animal biology assignments the painting of earth or shadow colors can also be encouraged, so that animals, even though we do not paint naturalistically, really find themselves in and on the earth. Connecting with the earth element is important for this age group.

In the Creation story from Norse mythology, we find motifs to complete this transition from soul mood to nature mood while painting. A foothold for the conversation with the children about nature moods is the difference between warmer and cooler colors, this combined with the four elements: earth, water, air and warmth / fire. In fact the entire path to landscape painting rests on this. In the Norse Creation stories there are two worlds. "Niflheim" [Mistland] is the home of mist and darkness, cold and vast wastes, with even blowing icy winds. In "Muspelheim" heat reigns supreme, scorching and fiery, burning everything. Between these two areas is a deep chasm, the "Ginnungagap." The children paint the cold, chill colors on one side and the warm, intense heat colors on the other side. We can expand this image further in a second exercise. The children are given the task to paint these two worlds with different blue colors: the cool Prussian and the warm ultramarine. As a third exercise the two worlds are created with the two red colors. They make "warm and fiery" with the vermilion and find the icy, cold climate in the carmine, mixed with other colors (while keeping it predominantly red). With exercises of this kind the child develops subtle nuances of feeling. Surprisingly enough the children discover many a landscape in the results: heavier, earthy, cool below and the warmer above. But turn this painting upside down and it becomes even more impressive. From this sketch it becomes possible to set up color conversations about the landscape, landscape in warm and cold colors, in other words, landscapes in warm countries and landscapes in cold regions.

With the elements water, air and earth many landscape possibilities present themselves. Details are not important yet; the most important aspect is the mood in nature. Aspects such as time, season and place can be further developed in fifth and sixth grades, up to and including the weather conditions in seventh and eighth grades. The unity of the mood should always prevail. The colors must, no matter how harsh the contrast on a painting might be, form one whole, a natural whole. Trees and forests can still be omitted in fourth grade to let the children arrive at the landscape first out of the color rather than from too strong a representation. A lot depends on the teacher's choice of words. The landscape can be well described in dialogue with the children, especially when children have been to such a place; their experiences are important. After this conversation the moment arrives when this information can be "rethought" into color qualities. "Is it light, dark, warm, cold, pleasant or mysterious there? Is there perhaps a color available which holds within it the ground mood? Is this to be found in the purple/blue or more in the green/blue?" Similarly, in the local history or first geography lessons, the children go out to explore their own surroundings and they can travel around landscape colors during the painting lessons. What is observed is internalized and brought out again consciously during the painting lessons, an important pedagogical aid in training the thought processes.

Maps

In conjunction with the local history lessons in fourth grade, the first maps can be painted and drawn. It is interesting for the children to be able to view a number of examples, so they become aware of the historical development of the map form. The first maps for example, do not show a town as seen from above, but from the side. The mapmaker's standpoint is still on earth. Not until later will the landscape be painted or drawn from a bird's eye view. A map, as we know it today, full of color areas, line and symbols, is a little abstract to the pupil. Most pupils would need to go a long way before understanding a "proper" map.

The next exercise involves the stages describing how a bridge can be built between the known world of the child and the information we wish the child to understand gradually. This is done by means of a simple color series. This gives the pupil a hold on the meaning linked to the colors on the map.

As a first step we paint three colors with the children: yellow, green and blue. We position the colors one after the other. Now we ask the children to imagine what it would be like for them if they found themselves on that yellow part of the sheet. What sort of a landscape do they see? The pupils make their own descriptions. Now, as it were, we walk from the yellow to the green part. The pupils describe this trip in their own words. Finally we arrive at the blue part. What does that look like? In practice the pupils will write down different experiences and ideas. One pupil started this trip in a desert and reached the sea via an oasis. Yet another was in a small dune valley and walked to a lake via the woods. It is important for them to use their imagination as much as possible and if they can manage, to describe the surroundings and possible adventures in detail. In this way the pupil connects his own inner world with information from the outside. The previously chosen color series can now be replaced by a different series of three colors which we can find in the color circle, for example from purple via the red to the orange; or from the green via the yellow to the orange. The pupils will then also start describing mountainous landscapes, valleys and swamps. Descriptions of differences in temperatures and height and land use can also be covered. In this way the pupils orientate themselves, and other elements such as roads and towns can possibly be added. This way of working can be followed alongside the creation of their first maps, recorded as a result of concrete situations and information (class, school, direct environment). To conclude this colorful project the pupils could try to involve the entire color circle on a trip in their own surroundings or in distant lands.

When we explore the map of the Netherlands, painting is particularly suitable to pointing out its characteristic aspects. For example, we start from the historical development of our river areas, the course of the Rhine from high to low, from the color background above described or described from a position with a high horizon. For example from the "Gelderse Poort" where the Rhine enters Holland, we look at the sea and in this way the river areas spread out in front of us. Or we look in the direction of the Alps and the Rhine flows towards us. We could also be on the beach, with the sea behind us.

There are many possibilities for each child to express his own point of view. Then all facts can be processed, until the role of color has become a supporting one, the maps have become too detailed to paint with thick brushes, and the coloring pens take over the job.

Animal and human figures

The exercises linking up with the first animal biology lessons have to be set up in such a way, that out of the colors only those forms arise which express what is typical and characteristic of an animal. The essence of an animal species is important rather than its immediate outward appearance. How is it a bird can fly? Which elements are involved in this? What is the essence of the cow? We have to search for examples in such a way, that it becomes clear to the children how an animal lives and in which habitat, as well as its position and tasks in nature. In the course of the painting lesson, the children can experience how an animal's habitat is shaped by the different elements: cold, warm, air, light, water and earth. We first look for a ground mood and the corresponding colors. If we start with an octopus, we will describe the underwater world. "Who has had his eyes open while swimming under water? What can you see?" Different experiences from inland and foreign waters come up. The varied color play between light and darkness is called up as an image.

In this way the children can paint the entire sheet with tenuous, thin colors. Everything flows into each other, everything is in motion, without fixed shapes. In the midst of this the octopus moves. The remarkable aspect of this creature is that all colors are reflected in the large eyeballs. The green-pink like colors shoot across the long tentacles. Colorful clouds float across the belly. When we describe the creature like this, the children feel the need to paint it in this way. On the soft color tints foundation they can now start painting the octopus from the head. Different colors move in all directions. This is how the octopus comes about, while floating and swimming in a color bath. Of course octopuses will be painted who will have to fend off a supposed enemy. A dark ink-like cloud partly obscures the octopus from view.

The jellyfish is another semi-transparent water creature. It lets itself flow along with the movement of the water and shows wonderfully soft colors. It floats along flower-like, a solidified water mass. The fire jellyfish will be given some stronger accents by using red. All types of fish can also be painted on a delicate multicolored background. After some fish have been painted, the surroundings can be darkened, so that the light, mirroring quality of the scales can be expressed. The children submerge themselves deeply in the water element during these assignments.

When we paint the cow, completely different qualities play a role. The most essential parts of this animal are the enormous digestive organs. In fact, we could say that there is an enormous stomach lying there in that juicy meadow, masticating. Its body is at the mercy of gravity. Large scale, long term processes take place within the cow's digestive system. The animal has to eat its weight in food several times over in order to stay alive. The warmth organism is very strongly developed. Whoever has been inside a cow shed in winter, will have experienced how warm and humid the atmosphere is there. Human beings are also warmer in the abdominal regions (about a tenth of a degree) than in the head. The warmth necessary for the digestion of food is the most important element of the cow. The warmth can initially be painted with vermilion red across the entire sheet. Subsequently the animal itself can be painted from the curve of the rump.

Steiner describes how humans, unlike animals, have developed from the head. "With humans the head is first to evolve. The remainder becomes an appendage, which hooks itself, as it were, up to the head. Humans, in their cosmic evolution, grow from the head down. ... The human starts with the development of the head, then adds the chest, the chest metamorphosis, then in turn the digestive organs. The lion starts with the chest, then adds the head and then, simultaneously with the human during the noontime, he receives the digestive organ. The animals of which the cow is a representative, first build the digestive system and then growing from this the chest and head organs are seen. So you see: The human grows from the head down, the lion from the chest upward and downward, and the cow, so to say, compared with the human entirely upward, towards heart and head."

The cow is best painted in a recumbent position to work around the problem of the four legs. We paint the animal as big as possible to effect a clear and powerful color tone. Afterwards we can make the surroundings a delicious juicy green. The green automatically becomes slightly darker due to the red in the foundation colors (more on this in the botany section). Sky and horizon are not important. This would pull the children towards a naturalistic representation and would give the painting a depth which does not benefit the color tone. The spatial effect is evoked by the color areas, not the representation. One could of course paint lighter tints upwardly and especially under the cow darken the colors somewhat, for a free floating cow is definitely out of place. Finally the children can paint over the warm colors of the cow with a blue, so that calm and harmony become apparent. After all a cow is not a bull. Painting the eyes last is essential, however restricted one is when painting with the wet-on-wet technique. It shows the animal is an "ensouled" creature. Just like us it looks into the world.

Painting over the cow with blue (and any other animal) with blue requires further explanation. When we only paint the animals with the primary pure colors, they remain cosmic, angel-like creatures, not connected with the earth. Adding the blue, in particular, which is placed across the entire creature like a veil, reflects the earthly connection. The lustre character of the color is darkened by this veil. Steiner describes this process in relation to the distinction of colors in lustre and image colors.[13] More on this in Chapter 6. The pure colors are the lustre colors. They express their essence directly in the color, just as the sunlight gives us direct light and warmth. A blue on top of the lustre colors (blue on top of blue demands a different artistic technical solution) gives them image character. The new color has an indirect effect, like the image colors. The essence remains somewhat hidden to the eye and works, as it were, behind the color, as in the way we can experience the difference between sunlight and moonlight. The new quality, which then arises when painting animals, is called by Steiner *image lustre*. Blue represents the "lustre of the soul." Painting a thin blue layer breathes life into the animal, as it were. On the pure lustre color the blue has the effect of a shadow. It gives this color "image character." This theoretical background, described in more detail in Chapter 6 of this book, seems complex, but it can be applied in practice immediately with and by the children. Its effect is obvious and astounding. The children do not have to know the reasons behind it, of course. For them painting blue over the creature is sufficient.

We also find this application when painting birds, the eagle for example. Eagles can move freely in the air, using the warmth from

13. See Chapter 2 in Steiner's *Colour,* London: Rudolf Steiner Press, 1971.

their bodies in and between their feathers. The warm element is carried by the cooler surroundings. This is called "thermals." Without a single flap of the wing the eagles circle upward and the seagulls soar along the dune-sides. "The bird is, one could say, a warmth-air creature, for the true bird is the warm air extending within the bird; the other parts are the luggage it drags through this world."[14] The bird feels the air he draws in as its essence.

Schematically speaking, the bird actually feels as its essence that which penetrates it as air and spreads out over its entire body. This air spreading within it and warming it is its essence. Here, again, painting a warm color inside a cooler color is the most important. When this color tone has arisen, the children can start to paint the bird itself. From the small head with the curved beak the eagle spreads its enormous wings diagonally across the sheet. Yellow, golden yellow and orange colors appear. Next the surroundings are adjusted. The air element is strengthened here and there. How does the eagle continue to give the impression of flying or floating rather than falling like a brick?

How do the colors really support one another? The secret in this is that when the bird's surroundings are colored more weightily, the colors are propelled in an upward direction. This effect could be intensified by stronger colors for the bird itself. The children will have to try this themselves. Later on it can be observed which birds give the impression of flying and which ones find it hard to stay up in the air, possibilities galore for a discussion afterwards. Which go up and which come down? In conclusion, when we carefully paint over the plumage with blue strokes, beautiful brownish hues arise. This sun bird creature shines as if golden. The essence of the bird is

14. See Steiner's *Man as Symphony of the Creative Word,* London: Rudolf Steiner Press, 1995.

expressed this way in the paintings. This creates a direct link with the subject matter discussed in the animal biology lessons. Using colors artistically enriches the knowledge and the insight into the animal world.

The buildup of the colors and the method used for painting the animals mentioned above can be applied to all sorts of other animals as well. It is a matter of constantly following a series of logical steps: painting a ground mood in which the essence of the creature is expressed, the animal figure itself, adjusting the surroundings, and painting over the figure softly with blue so it will be included in the whole. No animal is dissociated from its surroundings after all. When painting a squirrel the fast movements can help in the choice of colors. Fox and mouse will be similar in this respect, and different in the case of the lion, the elephant or the camel. These animals are covered in the higher classes and are best painted then. Animals with special characteristics are rewarding subjects in the drawing lessons. Horns, beard, tail, neck, mane and hoofs are best done justice in the drawing lessons after proper observation. The teacher can always consider this when choosing a drawing or painting assignment.

Julius Hebing writes in his diary:

> Take in what can be observed in such a way that it outwardly enriches us inwardly. Not until then can a landscape, a flower or an animal painted as an image in such a way approach the spiritual reality. From the inside it is born anew and passed on in a changed form.[15]

---

15. From Julius Hebing, *Lebenskreise –Farbenkreise,* not yet translated into English.

When we return to the stories, the painting of figures, as started in third grade, can now be further expanded. The gods with their various characteristics lend themselves perfectly for colorful work. Odin with Freya, Thor with his hammer, the sly Loki. One of the most exciting moments is the shooting of the arrow by the blind Hodur to his brother Balder while Hodur is supported by Loki. The children will find the colors for these figures without much difficulty.

The surroundings can be adapted around the gods in many colors. The rainbow with Heimdal, the guardian of the Bifrostbridge between the realm of humans and gods, is a favorite for the children to paint.

Initially themes from Norse mythology are best painted in clear colors and sufficiently strong where the moods so require. The Ugdrasil and Bifrostbridge continue to be dreamlike images. The landscape tends toward black in the battle of the gods; this is an important moment for the fourth grade pupil.

* Basic exercise #7a for the teacher

From the painting of nature moods it is necessary to explore the area of the grey- and brown-like colors. Up until now the children have painted predominantly with the three primary colors and the accompanying mixed colors, the secondary colors. There is however a large group of thrilling colors containing the three pure colors: the tertiary colors, also referred to as "earth colors." In order to obtain a multitude of different earth colors in one go, we can do the following exercise, a so-called "passing on exercise." This exercise is necessary before one starts teaching a fourth grade. This is how it is done:

The three primary colors yellow, red and blue are painted in three equal areas on the sheet, at the top, bottom right and bottom left. The colors stand right next to each other without space in between.

Now, yellow (the paint of the sheet) is painted into the red (rinse the brush), the blue color on the sheet we paint into the yellow (rinse the brush), and with a little red paint from the jar (because the red on the sheet has already become orange through the mixing with the yellow), we paint into the blue. All three pure colors have now shifted and the three mixed colors have arisen: green, orange, and purple. Now we also work with these three new colors, initially without dipping again. The green we paint into the orange, the orange into the purple and the purple into the green.

The aim is to paint as much as possible with the colors on the sheet, but where we have too little paint on the sheet we can take this from the painting jars. Now all sorts of tertiary colors are created: brown- and grey-like. Theoretically speaking, the same color should arise in each situation. After all, all the colors spring from the same yellow, blue and red. But practice shows that by a different order of application and through the lively painting process, a wealth of colors becomes possible. Not everyone immediately recognizes this wealth. After the experiences with the bright beaming colors, these new colors do not always come across as pleasant. But by working with them for awhile one can soon distinguish more and more nuances. In fact the double mixed colors actually "shine up" the single ones. It takes time to learn to appreciate them and to find them "beautiful." The children sometimes refer to them as "autumn colors" and sometimes find it hard to see their value. "Bah, dirty poo colors," one child says. "I'll just have yellow and red!" The path towards the grey tints is a painful one for some. However, we need these colors for painting night moods and the habitat of creatures living close to or below the ground.

* Basic exercise #7b for the teacher

The following basic exercise is a preparation for landscape painting in fifth grade and beyond, when we link up with the creation story in Norse mythology (Muspelheim and Niflheim).

Cut a (standard format) sheet of painting paper in three, producing three equally oblong pieces. Lay them one below the other. The theme for these three paintings is landscape.

We choose two colors for each sheet: for the top sheet lemon and golden yellow, for the middle sheet vermilion and carmine red, for the bottom sheet ultramarine and Prussian blue, a warmer and colder tint of one color for each sheet. Now we paint one of the two tints on the upper half of the oblong sheet and the other color on the remaining bottom half. It does not matter really whether one starts with lemon yellow at the top or golden yellow. Both varieties can be tried out. The dividing line between the two colors does not necessarily have to be straight; it quickly works as a horizon line. When all six colors have been applied to the sheets one can freely choose which colors with which one wants to carry on working. With small color areas mountains, clouds, lakes, trees, and so forth, can now be simply indicated. It is important to make sure that the initial colors continue to dominate.

When the landscapes are finished, they will give three completely different impressions. The aim of this exercise is to learn to observe how these different colors give expression to nature moods and how crucial warmer or colder colors are in determining the mood of a landscape. The above exercise can also be done with two green, two orange or two violet colors. Various combinations are also possible. One keeps on reaching a different place on earth, a different climate or time of day or year.

This basic exercise helps us to view the color circle from the soul moods and allows us to connect the colors with the four elements: earth, water, fire/warmth, light and air, to take the path from soul moods to nature moods. When one gives these elements a position around the circle, writes them down, and links them to the four wind directions, one can arrive at the following division: Between orange and red is South, opposite this between blue and green is North, between the green/yellow, West, and violet/red color East. Between East and South the fire element, warmth. Between South and West the earth element, which can also be experienced as dryness. Between West and North the air/light element, and finally between North and East, wetness. Thus, warm and cold, wet and dry stand opposite in the circle. We can use this color circle to orient ourselves to the nature moods. We can then apply this to landscapes in the higher classes of primary school.

2.7 Painting in the fifth grade

Experiencing processes

In fifth grade horizons are broadened. In the botany lessons plants, flowers and trees are now discussed. The plant world forms a thin vulnerable layer between heaven and earth. Form, color and growth of plants are dependent on the local conditions. The roots nestle into the earth, stem, leaf and flower grow upward towards the sun. Sunlight and warmth are essential to plant life. The plant moves between earth's darkness and heaven's light, an upward ambition despite gravity. Flowers take on all shades of color, spread scents, and their seeds float on the wind. This world gains the interest of the ten-, eleven-year old pupil. We can observe developments in the different plant types related to the phases of development of the growing child. The toadstools grow in the lap of the earth, only a small part of the plant looks out above the earth. The fern unfurls its leaves slowly but surely. In a series of examples the pupils can see and experience that the plants develop and become more complex, even to a woodifying process in the stem of the roses. In the shapes of flowers the children discover five- and six-petaled stars. In the way leaves are attached to the stem, or in the heart of a sunflower, they even find spiral shapes.

Everything in the plant world is created, grows and flowers between the polarity of light and darkness. The spring sun draws the first fresh green (Greek: *chloros*) from the branches. In the summer sun the greenery becomes heavy and saturated. In the autumn the summer warmth expresses itself once more with bright colors in the leaf, before returning to the earth, extinguished, while fruits and seeds guarantee the perpetuation of life through the winter months. These processes recurring yearly in nature are the source of inspiration for our artistic work. In fifth grade we are not concerned with a schematic representation of plants, or their analysis. The children should be able to experience the plant as one with its environment and that it is made up from the four elements. The course of the plant year is a closing circle, but also an upward spiral of development. Living and dying are closely linked. From the seemingly dead new life germinates.

Plants and trees

The children can witness the processes of plant life while painting. Darkness below and the beaming light above. The color yellow, making the light visible to our eyes, on the one side and blue, the first color to be created when lighting up the darkness, on the other side. It is still important, however, to paint the soft carmine red over the entire sheet to begin with, just like we did with the creation images in third grade: The warmth, from which everything is created, spreads calmly across the entire sheet . Then yellow will shine through this from top to bottom and meet the blue painted from the bottom up. In the middle a darker green automatically appears, darker than any mixed from blue and yellow, due to the red. We link directly with Steiner when he says that the plant character of the green is only shown to its full advantage if it is painted darker than it really is. This is how the plant green is created. There is a close relationship between the plant and the color green. The word green is related to the old Germanic word *gehre* which means to germinate, or the process of growing. In our Dutch and English the words *groen/ green* and *groeien/growing* are phonically linked.

The green we observe in the plant world is not the most essential part of the plant, that is the living, the growing element. This living element itself has a different color, red, which Steiner calls "the lustre of life." The green is an image of this, not of life itself. "Green is the lifeless image of life." The red points of new shoots on plants and trees are remarkable in the spring. This living "lustre" element withdraws, as it were, as summer approaches and the plant dies gradually in the heavier green. A beech forest in the early spring also shows this pink glow through the foliage. After some weeks a green shadow falls on this and the red does not return until the autumn as a last sign of life. Red is the lustre of life and green the lifeless image of life. (see Chapter 6.1)

We make this idea concrete by painting red "under" the yellow and blue. Prussian blue gives a clearer, colder green than the ultramarine, which contains a lot of red, warmth. From the latter color we can create the moss-like greens. An entirely different color tone comes out when the blue is above the green and the yellow below. Downwardly more red can be painted to create earth colors with the blue and yellow. More blue in the painting provides a humid climate, red reinforces the warmth element, and yellow the light element. The children try out all these elements in the painting lesson to discover, in this way, the various ways of creating green. The eighth basic exercise for the teacher can also be done by the pupils to explain the plant green. Out of the color, leaf and stem can be created simply, without having to draw. Forms automatically appear where lighter greens stand next to darker greens. When we strengthen the warmth element in the air/sunlight part of the painting, the pupils make the flowers appear as if by magic: first the red, orange and yellow and finally the blue and purple. A flower is a climax, a concentration point of warmth and a certain end point in the appearance of the plant before it goes to seed. Different types of plants can also be appropriately painted in the sixth and/or seventh class. The dandelion remains a marvelous example to paint in the botany lessons in fifth grade: root, leaf, stem and shining yellow flower.

When discussing trees with children during a botany lesson, Steiner expressed himself thus, "Look, imagine that plant next to this tree. What does this tree look like then? Yes, it has roots at the bottom, certainly, but then there is not a stem but a trunk. Then it spreads out its branches and it almost seems as if on the branches actual plants grow. For on those branches are leaves and flowers, small plants. We can see a meadow in a completely different light; across the meadow yellow buttercups grow. The meadow is covered in plants, all having their roots in the soil. But with a tree, it is as if one has picked up the meadow, lifted it up and bent it round, so that all those flowers started growing up there. The trunk itself is a piece of earth. The tree is the same as the meadow in which the plants grow."

The step from painting a plant to painting a tree is a small but an important one. With a tree, the trunk pushes up the earth element and the foliage is created in the air/light element. We need not consider a special type of tree at this stage because many types appear in the children's work. We are mainly concerned with the process of becoming, so therefore the seasons can be focused upon, as well as the various stages of the tree. It is important to discuss the proportion of trunk to crown, otherwise we will still get to see many "toddler trees": thick trunks with small crowns. A little tip to give the tree a more shining, so more living, character is to paint the tree's surroundings darker. This makes the leaves light up. Blossoming trees in spring can be painted by using many delicate colors. The children will discover that each color change produces a different tree in a different season.

To round this off, here is another description by Steiner:

> There is the sun. The sunlight falls on the tree. Now one should not start from the tree and draw, but one should start from the light areas and dark areas, so that the tree is created from this contrast of color, coming from the light. Not to start with the abstraction: the tree is green. Do not let the leaves be painted green; the leaves should not be painted at all. Light areas should be painted.[16]

Mythology, history and maps

In fifth grade the Greek mythology stories are told. Many adventures of gods and heroes file past. This atmosphere surrounds the fifth grade pupil. As the year progresses it becomes clear from

---

16. See Steiner's *Conferences with the Teachers of the Waldorf School in Stuttgart, Volumes 1, 2, 3,4,* Forest Row, England: Steiner Schools Fellowship Publications, 1989.

the stories that people become more and more in control, as the gods withdraw to holy Mount Olympus. This transition is often accompanied by shocking events. After all, Zeus wishes to be all-powerful and wants to carry on controlling the course of divine and human life. The predictions, which play a large part in various stories (for example, in the story of Oedipus), refer to ancient clairvoyant abilities. The world of the gods has to yield its position to the world of people. The freedom of choice in how to live comes to the front. Sports are a central part in the Greek civilization: a healthy mind in a healthy body. This harmonious image is also typical of the fifth grade pupil. After growing in height and mass their bodies give an athletic impression. At school the fifth grade pupils are clearly distinguishable from the pupils in the higher classes who can give a clumsy, gawky impression due to their fast growth.

Many figures from Greek mythology are excellent for painting assignments. Cleverness, strength, despair, revenge, all sorts of soul conditions weave through the motifs of heroic feats. A class discussion provides ample color material to get started with. Mood, figure, surroundings and further individual developing (of the painting) remain the steps in the buildup. For this reason the teacher should encourage sharp color contrasts, color nuances and imaginative forms.

The ancient civilizations, from the Indian to the Egyptian and Greek cultures, are discussed and further worked out in the main lessons. Anything to do with ornament, decoration and architecture comes to its own in drawings. Working out of the color area in painting is not always suitable for these subjects. However, themes from the many stories related to ancient cultures are very suitable for class painting. Subjects such as ornaments, sculptures, temples, and so forth, are well-suited to group work; they can be painted colorfully and with different media in large format and they can cover the walls for the time of the main lesson blocks. This work can inspire the class and evoke an impression of the enormous structures that were built during these civilizations.

The maps of Egypt and Greece provide suitable painting assignments, for example, the Nile, with which the entire Egyptian civilization is very closely linked, flowing through the infertile desert landscape, a blue/yellow exercise in which fertile land springs up along the river, also the delta near the Mediterranean. Mountains can be painted with orange and red, so that the contrast of the Nile valley with the rough desert areas becomes visible from the color.

The map of Greece is very different with its thousands of kilometers of erratic coastline, rocks or beach, water around land. The redness of the rocks contrasts with the blue wavy sea in a powerful color tone. This is reinforced by the large groups of islands and the high inland mountains.

Thus the children experience the totally different characteristics of these two countries. The civilizations that came about in these countries confirm these mutual differences. When a country or a continent has enough color qualities within it, working on it in the painting lesson gives us many more possibilities than in the drawing lesson. We are talking about the qualities and the color of the polar forces from which the landscape or the form arises.

In this way we can also paint maps with the climate becoming visible in color. On the European continent, for example, different climate zones meet: from the West the blue, from the North the green, purple and blue; from the South the warmer tints red, yellow and orange, and from the East a red from below and a blue from above, creating a purple. They can meet on a yellow applied as a foundation. It becomes a lively whole, in which mountains and lower regions by the seas are expressed together with the climate spheres. Maps can be well- painted up to eighth grade.

Landscape, animals and color perspective

The basis from which landscapes are painted is the difference between warmer and colder colors. Bearing this in mind, morning, evening and night moods can be discussed with the children. Is the earth in the evening after sunset cooler or warmer than the air? The air always cools down quickly in the evening, while the earth retains the warmth longer. The earth even releases "vapors," which we observe as mist clouds and trails in the landscape and above the water. At daybreak rather the reverse happens. The air is quickly heated by the sun, while the earth is still cold from the night.

The children distinguish the alternating warm and cold and determine their choice of colors with this in mind: Prussian or ultramarine blue? Lemon or golden yellow? Carmine or vermilion red? In the night mood the indigo is effective. Prussian blue with a little cinnabar red gives a beautiful cool, dark tone, in the pale white/yellow moonlight. Is there water, reflecting the moon or an open space in the woods with many shadows?

With the children place, time and country can be discussed each lesson, sometimes also linking up with the geography lessons. A basis or foundation color on which further painting can be done can yield special effects, for example, painting on a vermilion red foundation. The children imagine themselves straightaway in warm, tropical lands. In sixth and seventh grades these assignments can include such extreme areas.

In the lively description of far foreign regions the animal can take its place. The format for the assignments with animals is the same as that used in fourth grade. The African elephant can be set up from the blue, in a jungle environment, the camel from the golden yellow. With a blue veil the figures emerge in warm brown tints. Owls painted in brown and grey colors turn up magically from an indigo-like night mood. Let the children paint the animals on a large scale with characteristic colors. "What are the conditions like, where have you seen one?" Try to include the pupils' own experiences in the assignments. The relationship with the artistic process is strengthened this way, and the children will feel more involved, even if, so to speak, only one child has seen a certain creature and has been able to talk about it.

Working out of the color and the area remain important even now. Depth, the three-dimensional effect in the painting, stems from the working of the different color areas. Some colors yield, some colors come forward. Children are easily inclined to make one side dark, especially when painting mountains. It has a remarkable effect, but it emphasizes the working of light and shadow, which is covered later in black and white drawing. The children will have to try and aim for this depth effect by using different colors, giving rise to so-called color perspective. We find marvelous examples of this in the work of many Impressionists (e.g., Cezanne). Perspective created through color gives a fullness to the color and places the landscape in an exciting color tone. This contrasts with the bareness of a contrived optical effect.

When the children, or even just part of the class, are strongly inclined to set up the images from the graphic or light/dark, the teacher can dig up all sorts of varied color exercises from previous years to let the children let go and immerse themselves into colors. One can satisfy the need for graphic representation by engaging them in sketching exercises. Painting and drawing work in different spaces—areas opposed to lines. In landscape painting both elements are too easily incorporated. It is possible to discuss ways of working separately with both elements thus simplifying matters.

Annual festivals

From the third grade onward color tones can already be painted which are linked directly to the seasons: light red with green and yellow (spring mood) or golden yellow, red/orange and blue (autumn and winter moods), as yet without any particular images. These are covered in fourth grade, e.g., the Madonna with Child, the three Kings, Saint Michael and the Dragon, children with Martinmas lanterns, the Saint John's night fire. The children discuss the color mood and soon enough the figures leap out in a lively interplay of colors.

* Basic exercise #8a for the teacher

In order to experience the difference between green (as a mixed color of blue and yellow) and plant green more clearly, this exercise shows the two next to each other.

Paint the center of the bottom part of the sheet a soft carmine red, increasing slightly in strength as you go down. Now from one side, you paint the entire width with yellow and from the other side similarly with blue. In the middle, from top to bottom, green is created through mixing yellow and blue. On the bottom, however, a different green is created, because this has a red foundation. This green has a deeper, darker effect. Painting again with carmine red, the contrast with the green above becomes even sharper. The image color green is created, whereas the top green is still a lustre color. The upper green is Steiner's green with a lustre character. To be able to experience and see this, the above exercise should really be executed in the veil technique rather than the wet-on-wet.

Next we take one step further. After the image color green has been created, the green becomes rather lifeless. After all, green is the lifeless image of life. To give it a lively character, reflecting nature, a few veils of yellow/ white can be painted over the green. This gives the image color lustre again and a green with a "lustre image" quality is created. In summary: The lustre colors yellow and blue give green its lustre character. Red darkens the green to a shadow color, an image color. Through the lustre effect and the quality of yellow/white a lively green is created, or lustre image. We recall the assignment with the animals in which we painted a blue veil over the lustre character of the animal figure; first there was lustre quality, and, by means of the blue, the image character was given image lustre. This is in contrast to the process taking place in the plant world, an ensouled world as opposed to an inanimate one.

* Basic exercise #8b for the teacher

After discovering the big difference between plant green and green (blue and yellow), we can greatly vary the number of first exercises with the children, linking up with the botany lessons.

When painting plants we can cover the entire leaf with a soft carmine red, the color of warmth as a basis for life, described by Steiner as the substance related to the Saturn epoch, a number of phases before the current earth development. After this thin veil of red, we follow with the colors yellow and blue to make green. We link the light/ air element with the elements of earth and water. In this first exercise the underlying red has an even effect through all colors. In the next few exercises we can, so to speak, place accents with the carmine red color. For example, by making the upper half of the painting stronger with this color than the bottom part, so eventually creating a warm tint, we can intimate a different season, in which the air is warmer than the earth. Likewise we can paint the middle or bottom part of the paper with a more powerful red. In the first case the plant green will have a warmer tint and more of a brown-green color. When there is more red in the earth/water area, the earth glows and brings about other color combinations. Here we can think of autumn or late afternoon. This shift in accent changes the mood. Here we can think of different types of soil and landscapes, with their own color ranges.

The above exercises can also be combined with other locations for the yellow and blue. After the red we can also start at the top with blue and place the yellow below, thus creating a completely different image, the green with blue at the top and yellow at the bottom. This basic exercise actually has six different variants, allowing us to discover many new color variants.

These color exercises constitute a good start to the botany main lessons, because it is not yet important which plant species we paint from the green. The plant is one with its surroundings. From the colors red, yellow and blue, a new world is created time and again, depending on the color strength and its location on the painting. Developing a feeling for the unity in nature precedes the knowledge of plant species and parts making up the whole of the plant.

Consequently the botany lessons can be combined quite successfully with color exercises, executed with wax crayons or blackboard chalk.

In a lecture on lustre and image colors Steiner says:

So, if you want to paint a landscape with plants
and trees and you want it to make a true natural
impression, you should make the green, as well as the
other colors, somewhat darker than the plant itself.
One should always paint a green area darker than

it is in nature. The red and the yellow in the plant world should, equally, be a little darker. And after we have recorded the color in its image character in this way, and given it a deeper tone, we should apply a certain mood to the whole, a sort of yellowish white color nuance. We should place the entire painting in a yellow-white light, not until then will the plant show up properly. A lustre should be painted over the image-character.[17]

It is not so important that we cannot yet take this last step with the children because they do not use the veiling technique but the wet-on-wet. Because the work is wet during the entire painting process, the lively "illumining" is amply expressed and the green approaches the true plant green. Terms such as "image" and "lustre" are not used with the children. (see Chapter 6.1)

2.8 Painting in the sixth grade
On the path to exact observation

Characteristic of the sixth grade curriculum is the subject of physics. From the areas of light, sound, warmth, magnetism and electricity simple themes are chosen. These awaken the intellectual abilities of the children, not by imparting abstract knowledge to them, but by letting them discover laws and formulations on the basis of dozens of experiments. From a pedagogical point of view, the following method is used. The class sees or does a number of experiments. No one speaks during the experiments. Watching and observing, eyes and ears, yes, all senses open to what is happening in class. After everything involved with the experiments has been

17. See Steiner's "The Hierarchies and the Rainbow," January 4, 1924, in *Colour*, London: Rudolf Steiner Press, GA 291, twelve lectures, 2001.

put away, the teacher discusses with the class what was seen and observed. The teacher should withhold any judgments, letting the pupils say only what they have seen and not what they think they have seen!

The next day the observations are recapitulated, but now from memory, and together conclusions can be drawn. The observations and the explicit conclusions are written in the main lesson book and the experiment is copied as accurately as possible, each day a little training in observation, remembering, rational research and recording. The children enjoy the causal connections and the emerging logic. By the way, this is only the very beginning of a long term process. Noticing and experiencing abstractions is not quite the same yet as being able to deal with them. The children do start to relate to other phenomena and to find ways of applying these in their own world. This process is a wake up call. The child becomes more certain of what he sees, thinks, and concludes. He learns to make a self-judgment. Judgments imposed too much from the outside at this age would create a make-believe world which would cause alienation from his surroundings. Building a bridge to the world with new, self-built foundations is important to twelve-year-olds.

The light and darkness experiments connect well with the painting lessons. After all, the pupils are quite familiar with the colors and will be surprised that on the basis of the experiments, color series and patterns are now made visible. The light is obscured with, for example, layers of sandwich wrappers: light yellow, yellow, orange yellow, even red. "The sandwich wrapper was white, wasn't it?" some wonder. The children are looking at a black piece of cardboard with a container of clear water in front of it. This water receives a strong light from the side. Now for some coffee cream in the water, stir it and a bluish shine stands out from the black background. The first lighting up, before the darkness, gives blue. Complementary colors are evoked in the pupils. They look through prisms and enthusiastically discover the wonderful color near windows and lamps. A well built up series of experiments leads the children through the entire color circle, and finally the colored shadows. "I can see them, so shadow obviously does not have to be black. But how is that possible?" These experiments are further explained in Chapter 6.

This elaborate description of a section of physics in sixth grade shows how the children begin to look differently at color. They become more aware, more critical, and will have more understanding of the (reciprocal) relationships of color. From this moment onward, every painting exercise, no matter how simple, is interesting again, as if they are doing it for the first time, new adventures which evoke that feeling of first grade again, so to speak. The curriculum for this class and that of seventh and eighth grades have been structured in relation to this awakening new critical capacity.

Minerals and the veiling technique

A new subject and a new technique meet the demands the sixth grade pupils now make. The pupils literally dive into the earth and discover the mineral world, the crystallized shapes, a world in which the light lustre, despite the complete darkness, radiates anew through rocks. Rocks are connected with the cosmos, with the stars, beaming from the dark skies at night. Minerals brought into class are regarded with great surprise: crystal, quartz in all colors and shapes. Can we paint this? Exercises are done in the wet-on-wet technique. We manage to express the mood, but specifically those crystallized forms and areas are unsatisfactory because of the damp method. "Children, today we are going to stretch thicker paper than usual on our painting boards. We wet the paper on both sides and make sure it is nice and tight on the board. Now we each take four strips of paper tape, wet this on one side and stick the paper down by attaching approximately one-third of the tape onto the white paper and the rest of it onto the painting board. Press the tape from the center to the outside, at the top and the bottom of the paper and left and right. Now we have to wait until tomorrow."

The next day the paper is nice and tight. Paper that has dried too quickly or is not attached properly could be partly loose. Because of the drying process the paper contracts and pulls on the tape—it becomes stretched. If there are some traces of grease on the board, the tape may not stick very well. To avoid disappointments it would be useful to stretch a few extra sheets, because everyone wants to get started straight away.

To make the process of veiling clearly visible, we choose a very watered-down Prussian blue. A blue haze becomes visible on a piece of testing paper. "Now we must make a habit of painting as dry as possible." How can you do that, as dry as possible with wet paint?" a pupil rightly asks. "Well, dip your wide brush (preferably #20 or wider) into the paint and wipe it well. We start with painting one area in one of the four corners. Start on the sticky tape, so you can see at once how much paint you have got on your brush. The most important rule is: You can paint only once on the same spot when veiling, otherwise you will brush away the bottom layer or dissolve it. That would make it wet-on-wet painting again. We paint an area with a straight boundary. But do not paint the way you would paint a door. Use small brush strokes in all directions. Keep it lively, but paint in such a way that on the outside of the area a straight boundary is being created. No, not yet with an edge in it. And here is another ground rule: Dip in only once for each area. Imagine you are halfway through painting one area and you take new paint. Splash, a big puddle in the middle of the sheet. Use all the paint on one brush per area. Now we can make areas in the other three colors, without these overlapping." The children can repeat this many times. "I find it quite difficult with all those restrictions." "Yes, but it does look good," one can hear the class say. "You can only start painting a new area when the paper is dry as a bone again. Be strict with yourself and check it by letting the light fall on the sheet from an angle. Is it shiny? And here is another tip: It will become tremendously boring if you paint over the same area twice. Make every area a little different!"

When the children have become familiar with the initial stages, they can expand the areas. From the corners now we have areas with blunt edges, then sharp edges. The control of the water on the paper is gradually becoming more difficult for the children. Only a little white is left in the middle. Now we can paint areas loosely in the middle of the sheet. The painted work is now covered with transparent areas. A crystalline world has been created. We can continue to work on it each day, for example, the first thirty minutes of main lesson. If the children still work with too much wet and the drying process consequently takes longer, the teacher can tell a story in the meantime or other work can be done. After four or five layers it becomes obvious that the new "veils" no longer "contrast" as much with previous areas.

Then the time has come to increase the strength of the paint somewhat. When the sheet is full of color, we are going to apply darker areas from the outside in, so that a radiating inner world is created. The more darkness, the stronger the light shines. Searching in the painting, the children leave open spaces for the crystal forms. A glance at all the work gives the impression that the tables are covered with enormous diamonds. The surprise grows when the dried work is cut loose with a sharp knife between the paper and the board and then framed under a white matte board. The dirty tape is gone, the color shows up wonderfully, and the crystal lights up.

The veil technique has to be learned step by step. It should not really fail. Patience is tested. This process has corresponding features with the physics lessons: The conclusion does not come until the next day. There needs to be space and time in the process. In this way the pupils are strongly confronted with work done the previous day. All veils remain visible. You carry on with this: observing, taking a distance, making decisions and continuing the work. There are fast, dry workers and wet and slow ones. Mistakes disappear from the paintings because of the many layers increasing in strength; very reassuring. For the next "veiling" more colors can be used. The children discover that this increases the degree of difficulty. Oddly enough yellow turns out to be an awkward veiling color. It radiates so much and is too easily applied too strongly. A subtle use of the light is essential.

Let the pupils clean their boards after they have detached their veiled painting. Each child should learn straightaway, that the tape comes off easily by keeping it wet with plenty of water. About ten minutes soaking and the tape is easily removed with a palette knife. In sixth, seventh and possibly eighth grades many other subjects can be painted using this technique: waving, water-like shapes, Gothic window shapes, cubic or building shapes, rock and hill formations and also color tones according to one's own imagination.

The children offer plenty of ideas. While "veiling" they find out that the colors become much stronger by means of this technique, especially when they are dry. Now it becomes possible to work on the color quality. Not all children will take this step at primary school level, but with careful encouragement they will go a long way. At the secondary level, from tenth grade onwards, they can pick up this technique once again. In addition to the veiling, the children can still do plenty of work on wet paper.

The creation of the different stone formations is discussed: igneous, metamorphic, and sedimentary rocks. The polarity between limestone and granite mountains can easily be set up with color, for example, stalagmite caves showing many colors in white lime rock. The following text can serve as a source of inspiration for the children:

> In the subterranean corridors
> Leading to vaults
> Sound without interruption
> A murmuring river.
> My newly lit torch
> Casts many a capricious shadow
> Reflects in the water
> In a mysterious way.
> Only now do I see the world
> In which I'm going to be
> So many colors
> To meet me, radiating
> As if rainbows
> Are always shining here
> I feel overwhelmed
> Whoever suspected this
> That so deep in the earth
> Secrets are hidden
> Which only reveal themselves
> When light shines around them?

Volcanoes with their fiery colors, combined with black-indigo colors or icy blue/green colors of the slowly moving glaciers between the permanent snow are thrilling subjects for the painting lesson for the sixth grade pupil.

Flowers, landscape, trees

The thread from the botany lessons in fifth grade is picked up again. We can follow the processes taking place in nature stage by stage in the painting lessons. The degree of difficulty increases in the next series of exercises. So these exercises are appropriate for sixth and seventh grades as well as eighth grade, dependent on the possibilities of the class in question.

To start off with the entire sheet is painted over with a light carmine red. The warmth, the etheric element, pervades the entire plant world. Now first we choose a flower color closely related to the (background) color, because the further away it is from this color (seen from the color circle), the harder this exercise will be. We are going to paint red roses. On the soft red we paint two to four red areas. This is where the flowers will be eventually. Now, around this, from top to bottom we paint the yellow, and from bottom to top the blue. This gives us the plant green. Subsequently the flowers are worked on with smaller areas. After that we paint the surroundings with large dark green areas. Generally speaking colors can become lighter as we go up.

This brings us to a red/green tone. Little painted stems are superfluous. "Just look at a bunch of flowers, or a rose bush, can you see them there?" In between the green the flowers grow. Each flower has its own character. This one has just budded, another is completely open. These differences are essential to the painting assignments. Otherwise the painting quickly deteriorates into a green with four equal red balloons in it. For the flowers to be absorbed into the green, the children always paint some of the flower color into the immediate surroundings, i.e., the green. A great deal of red will also be necessary to make the color green deeper. The children can develop this assignment quite individually.

The next assignment is painting yellow flowers, daffodils or sunflowers. The shapes of flowers can be prepared by the children in the drawing lessons: flowers seen from the front, from the side, half open and also wilted. The method remains the same: applying a foundation color of light red; painting the flower color and location; creating the plant green; and developing the flower and its surrounding. The brown heart of the sunflower comes about with a little blue and orange. In this way paintings can be created with blue harebells, purple monk's hood, orange lilies. It becomes exciting when we get to the white flowers. Here also we can start from a soft red foundation. When painting white, believe me, it is possible, the children use a little bit of each color. In a strongly painted surrounding these tints create a white effect: white lilies in green or on deep blue/green tints the water lilies, with their large floating leaves. It is remarkable to see how the children experience this. "Painting white, without white paint, is possible!"

As background information the teacher can study the directions given by Steiner on white as image color and the work of Frits Weitmann, who gives a practical interpretation of these directions.[18]

Plants and flowers are a fascinating subject. Brightly colored flowers from tropical climate zones link up with geography lessons. Perhaps it is possible to take the subject "flower and butterflies" in the higher classes. A flower is like a butterfly attached to the earth, and a butterfly is a flower detached from the earth, a beautiful link, summarized by Steiner.[19]

---

18. Julius Hebing: *Welt, Farbe und Mensch: Aus dem lünstlerischen Unterricht der Waldorfschulen*, not translated into English.
19. In German, *Wahrspruchworte* (*Truth-Wrought Words*), GA 40, now distributed in three titles by Steiner, *Breathing the Spirit, Finding the Greater Self*, and *The Heart of Peace*, all published by Rudolf Steiner Press, London: 2002.

For a renewed and exciting exploration of color in sixth grade, we refer you to basic exercise 7 for the teacher. This exercise can be painted in all its variations by pupils of this age group.

When painting landscapes with the sixth grade the weather conditions can be included: indigo black clouds, threatening above a tempestuous sea; thunder and lightning; many types of cloud, linking up with the study of the earth's atmosphere; rainbows in the landscape. These subjects, in turn, can be combined with nature through the different seasons. Mysterious, dark moods can also be created with the above mentioned exercise as described in the section for fourth grade (basic exercise 7a for the teacher). The light red in the set up of the primary colors is left partly without paint when passing it on to the mixed colors, and the earthly color, causing a brown-grey tone with red to emerge: a snatch of evening red after a misty rainy day. Many variants are possible. The children can work with this theme of painting over and over as freely as possible up to secondary level and beyond.

In the sixth grade various types of trees can be discussed with the children. A drawing assignment of an oak with its characteristic branch shapes can be a theme. Which ground mood/color do we choose for the oak? A powerful, obstinate element plays a part. Warm tints, with yellow and blue overlays, become the crown. Paint the trunk and some branches vermilion red. The surrounding should be darker rather than lighter to accentuate the strength. Then we take the beech, stately, its branches almost horizontally stretched into its surroundings. At the bottom of the beech tree hardly anything will grow; hence blue, purple tints in the design. Then the pale, almost silver birch, lively, sunny and light. The trunk, white-like, in a well-considered color mood, brings out the tender character of this tree. Then we have the weeping willow by the waterside, mirroring itself, stirring the surface of the water with its long branches, multiple nature moods. Each pupil has his own preference or feels somehow associated with one of the trees.

If the pupils in the higher classes are inclined to pin themselves down too much to a particular representation, which makes their paintings come out rather meagerly as regards color and form, the next exercise can bring back the fullness of the color. "Everyone, take a color in mind. Paint this color in the middle of your sheet. Which two colors are next to this one in the color circle? Keep that in mind. Choose one of those two. Paint this color in the top right and top left of your sheet. Now paint other colors going down along your sheet in the order of the color circle. At the bottom center of the sheet the colors are reunited. Now we apply the color, the missing link to the entire color circle, and which you had to keep in mind at the beginning of the exercise, to the remaining area in the center.

"Now to the right and the left you will see the complete color circle reflected. Because you started with all different colors, it looks completely different for many of you. Now the second stage. We paint from the outside with Prussian blue and save space for ground, trunk and crown-shape of the tree. We paint the blue in such a way that we can see how this color changes all the underlying colors. What type of tree has now come about? A certain type in a certain season? Develop this exercise further with different colors."

There is a large variety in the pupils' work: green spring trees against a dark background on a field dotted with yellow flowers, or an autumnal orange-like tree on a red/ purple ground, with a yellowish light shining through an ink-like Prussian blue. Everything has come about from one color exercise, first the doing, then the forming (leaving the open spaces), then the observation ("Hey, this is a …") and finally the working out. It can be refreshing for the sixth or seventh grade pupil to start with a different color at the top next time composing a totally different mood. ("How many possibilities are there anyway?")

Trees can be painted in many ways. The development of the painting is different for each pupil. If we link these four ways of working to the four seasons, it could look like this:

The spring tree. The entire sheet is painted with different light tinted small colored areas. Light red, yellow and blue areas are painted jointly, as if on a white sheet one has caught the blossom petals, which have been blown off by the wind and are fluttering in the air. With a blue we now paint the element of air and leave an open space for crown, trunk and earth. We keep on working from the outside to the inside, the left open form is given a chance to come out tentatively. We keep an eye on the crown-to-trunk proportion. Usually the trunk is made too big and too thick in relation to the crown. Subsequently the light tones of the crown are painted together with a soft red, so that one whole is created. The trunk can be painted darker now; the ground below and next to the trunk can then be adjusted to the whole. The pupils can make choices themselves, keeping the spring theme in mind.

The summer tree. This tree can be painted from the processes taking place in nature. We start off with the warmth and let a soft carmine red spread across the entire sheet. Then comes the light: The yellow shines through the red. With the blue we work on the earth element at the bottom of the sheet; it grows, goes upwards to trunk and crown. Green comes about automatically. The surrounding area of the crown can now be strengthened with yellow. This stops the green of the crown from contrasting too much with the surrounding area, and there is no silhouette of the tree, but it appears from the (two-dimensional) color perspective, not from the (three-dimensional) light-darkness. The trunk and the earth can now be further developed by the children.

The autumn tree. From the color circle we let the orange come out of the center. Now we leave open space for the tree with the complementary color blue. The blue is given a lively character because of the different ground tones. The crown shines towards us autumn-like through the dark surroundings. Trunk and earth can also be painted in a colorful autumn mood on the basis of the already-present yellow and green tints.

The winter tree. Can we try to paint white? Small areas of light red, yellow and blue are painted next to and on top of each other. They continue to cancel each other's one-sidedness. A grey-white mood is created. On this foundation we can now paint a bare tree in Prussian blue. Find a characteristic pose of trunk and branches. Four or five specific branch shapes work better than many undefined ones. The blue is painted over with vermilion red, giving the tree an indigo tint. With paint from the tree itself, work can be done on the surrounding area as desired. A yellow area can reinforce the wintry mood or a red-orange suggesting a sunrise or sunset. Many possibilities present themselves.

If we put the four different painting formats in order, we discover that the spring tree initially came out of space left open from a large variety of soft ground colors, the summer tree slowly emerged from warmth and light processes with blue, the autumn tree was created from a double color circle and the winter tree was achieved by drawing, painting on the "white." The ways described are not exclusive to the four seasons of course, for example, the spring tree, seen as a tender green/yellow, can also be created from the color circle, and so forth.

The highest classes of primary school can make calendars from these series, in which each season is portrayed with its own color mood.

Leaving an open space

By "leaving an open space" I mean that by not doing something, something is created. To apply this technique one needs overview and foresight. Forms are thus created by exploring. As yet invisible forms are created with color. This involves a degree of difficulty which can be an appropriate challenge for from pupils from sixth grade onwards. The skill of "leaving open spaces" of a particular area is very closely related to the release of the astral body. It is an indirect way of visualizing something. So, from observation, taking a distance, it becomes possible for the pupil in the course of the creative process to leave blank spaces to be filled in later. Going through this process in third or fourth grade would ask too much of the pupils.

Which subjects present themselves? The children think first of a swan, painting the entire sheet full of soft tints and then leaving the blank space with a darker color. "A flamingo, with such an amazing pink color." "Then a polar bear should be possible too," another one growls. "Why all these soft colors, I want something stronger!" "You can all paint small brightly colored areas next to each other today," says the teacher. "What is it going to be?" "Wait and see." A multicolored collection becomes visible in class. "Now we take a powerful Prussian blue and leave a blank space for a … parrot." Commotion in the class and these gaily, brightly colored feathered friends come forward large scale on the sheets, as if they are in the middle of a rain forest on branches entwined with liane vines. "You think about it this week, what else is possible? We will paint the nicest one all together next time."

Indigo

In sixth grade the need for precision arises and subsequently the need for perspective. Both areas can be given attention in drawing. "Leaving blank spaces" in painting can satisfy the desire for strong forms. Strong and intense colors, increased contrast between light and dark, or a three-dimensional effect can be achieved by working with indigo. Not only the history of the dye which produces this color but also its introduction into painting exercises (where it is added as a seventh color to the other six) will open up a completely new range of possibilities.

After the impulse of the clear "veiling" which holds the light, the indigo has a formative effect, bringing shadows and obscuring. The sixth, seventh and eighth grade pupil is looking for just this effect. The teacher makes a framework for the class, in which the new (material) is introduced step by step. The powers of the imagination from childhood can thus remain active in painting and be given a boost by means of the indigo, the color created by mixing vermilion red and Prussian blue.

2.9 Painting in the seventh grade
Exploring new worlds

The assignments for this class are a continuation and an elaboration of tasks brought in sixth grade, where a great deal was offered to the pupil, that now calls for further developing. There are large differences per class and per pupil. Landscapes, trees, plants and flowers can be worked out at varying levels appropriate to the individual. After their first "veiling" experiences, children want new subjects on which to work. The skills to paint layer after layer, to muster patience and to make the right choices are improving. With the painting of maps, as described in fifth grade, the children travel the world. Stories are told in seventh grade of the voyages of discovery to all corners of the world. New areas are being explored. Vivid imagination turns into reality or disappointment for many an explorer.

Each step takes a lot of energy from the seventh or eighth grade pupil. Where is the obvious? A turbulent stage of insecurity starts. The girls especially shoot up in height. The boys lag behind a little and compensate for this often with increasing quick wit and (quasi) maturity. Full of awe, they look up to the secondary school pupils. Emotional capabilities are strongly internalized and protected. Outwardly these are often expressed bluntly and with feelings of shame. When painting, their uses and choices of color can sometimes be very powerful and glaring.

Heavenly phenomena

In the lower classes, while painting night moods, there were little or no questions about the positions and movements of the moon. It was such a natural theme that it presented no problems at all. It was just a sickle-shaped or full moon. Now it is different. After all, when is it full moon? It is that sickle-shape that gives us problems. "We are going to paint an evening mood. The sun has just gone down. Like last night, when the sky had such a beautiful red afterglow with purple and blue streaks. At that moment the moon was already up. We are going to paint the moon as well. As a ground color we take a soft yellow tint, so that the moon can be painted out of this. Now the vividly colorful evening tints. We leave an open space for the moon. But what shape is the moon? What is its position? Is it first or last quarter now?" The pupils try to remember. They want to understand and explain their answers: "With the round side towards the sun, which shines on that part." The earth is painted strongly in the evening twilight. This is also a nice assignment to do with parents on parent evenings. Straightaway a third of the little moons face the other way. Usually we hardly stop at the thought of these phenomena, but after a number of observations in the evening with the class, the children will know the details.

During the next lesson the full moon is again discussed. "Isn't it big when it is just coming over the horizon and in winter it makes a big arc before going down again at sunrise." Fortunately we can look at the last quarter during the morning in main lesson. Each day the moon "crawls" closer to the risen sun until it disappears. The morning mood is chosen by the children: vermilion, golden yellow / red mood with the landscape still shrouded in cool colors.

Then the starry sky is dealt with, yellow as a foundation. First paint the stars, then the night colors: Prussian blue and indigo, with vermilion towards the night black. Now the children wish to see their own star signs in the sky. The main lesson book is produced and Aries, Taurus and all the other signs are studied once again. "Do you remember that your star sign is high in the night sky six months after your birthday?" The next day they enthusiastically find their own painting. Some have captured the star sign recognizably well; with others it has become a nice collection of stars. By exploring the world and explaining it the pupil builds up a measure of security for the turbulent years ahead in adolescence.

Voyages of discovery

Those who travel have a lot of stories to tell: History, but geography in particular provide us with ample subject matter for painting. Explorers bring back new unfamiliar products with them from faraway countries and describe for the first time fantastic unknown regions. When we let the children submerge themselves in this subject matter, we can paint many of these "strange faraway lands." We can help by asking questions like: Is it dry there, warm, wet or cold?" From this we have the following combinations: dry-cold, dry-warm, humid-warm and humid-cold. Polar regions, rain forests and deserts are created out of the color. "Grounding" the sheet in the appropriate mood facilitates the buildup of the landscape. These assignments can be combined with the seasons and times of day, for instance, sunrise in the desert, night in the rain forest, polar lights in Alaska. We travel around the whole world and then, with our skills, we can paint the whole world, the globe, from the above-mentioned qualities of the elements. We are also painting maps again in which the continents derive their colors from the climate. This could lead to large-scale group-work. The pupils should feel they have working space enough in the various artistic disciplines in which to come to a conscious managing of color and form.

The veiling assignments relate directly with the first experiences gained in sixth grade. Exercises can be repeated and expanded on as regards the colors. There is still plenty of experiences and discoveries by means of simple assignments.

Each teacher can pick up color inspiration from the human biology and the chemistry lessons. The science of nutrition provides a new avenue to the world of plants. Sour and sweet, salty and bitter can probably also be found in the color circle. Each link with color and form places the new subjects into a larger context. By means of lines and areas we can enrich the subject matter in the main lesson via the artistic subjects. In chemistry fire plays an important role. The flame of a candle shows nearly the entire color spectrum. The sometimes spectacular experiments call up excitement and drama in the color play. A seventh grade pupil likes to explore and redefine boundaries. Let him/her experiment within a clearly defined assignment. Individual differences in ability become more and more apparent. Independent research into colors can be encouraged through observational training, which will key into the physics lessons. For example, light and shadow can be explored by creating a color circle in a black made from all the other colors.

2.10 Painting in the eighth grade
Industrial activities and cultural landscapes

In eighth grade the painting curriculum is curtailed, because (for pedagogical reasons) in the next class little or no work is done with color. This is very closely linked with the major changes taking place in the lives of the pupils in this phase of development. During these years a multicolored inner emotional life springs up. One could say the thirteen- or fourteen-year-old phase could be typified as a lessons in which the child followed the teacher and could accept him as an authority; now in this new phase the pupil is on his/her way to a freer relationship with the teacher. This phase is often characterized by the words of Steiner, "Everyone should choose his own heroes, whom he meets on the way to the top of Mount Olympus." In prepuberty the pupil experiences radical change. Strong emotions swing this way and that; everything has to be different. From the way they dress to the decorating of a room—childhood "color" no longer rules. State of mind now holds sway as major physical change also occurs.

The individual soul life thus starts to connect itself more deeply with one's own physical body. This causes a more intense experience of self, self-awareness; feelings of loneliness often occur at this age. This is often expressed with the words: "Nobody understands me!"

To accommodate the changes taking place in the eighth grade pupil, some color exercises can still be repeated for sure, but made more demanding, including control of materials/equipment and technique. Working on a large scale can be a new challenge. Exercises in which darker tints are built up from powerfully applied primary and secondary colors can be especially rewarding.

It turns out again and again that not all pupils bring along their skills as natural luggage from sixth and seventh grades. Many of them have to struggle again to paint not too wet or too dry, for example. The inner changes are reflected in the way the pupils deal with painting. Sometimes they have to renew their search for what is possible. It is also remarkable that because of this the individual differences are very great. As regards this aspect, assignments turn out totally different: loud colors, dark and sharp next to results in soft, very subtly painted tints. Sometimes the urge to draw, to outline the areas becomes stronger for a number of pupils. The need for accentuation is great. This is why the teacher has to point out again how the same result can be achieved from the areas, from the two-dimensional.

Despite the fact that pupils have been working with these painting techniques and materials for eight years, we keep on noticing that working on the assignments is done with both concentration and pleasure. This is an age where the water jars are once again easily upset. The new and often strong physical development is undoubtedly partly responsible. It is important for the teacher to guide the lessons with enthusiasm. Some pupils do tend to choose the easy path and say, "I think we've covered this by now." After the first brush strokes, however, it turns out the reverse is true. Once they have started, they become involved again.

The pupils, during this lessons more so than in previous years, pay much more attention to the results of fellow pupils. Some pieces of work are not really admired until after the lesson. "How did you manage to do that?"

If the veiling and the working with indigo have been covered in sixth and seventh grades, then in this class we can emphasize subjects which are a challenge and which are also interesting from a painting point of view. Geography offers such subjects. Exploring nations and cultures can be reflected in landscape and climate paintings, in which the accent is now on people: house construction, town silhouettes, clothing, language, and so forth. All these subjects require a sense of the appropriate color surroundings and detail. The pupils like to focus on the task at hand. This is why it is important to link the assignments regularly with the main lesson subject matter.

In this way we can make a wonderful series of paintings in eighth grade around the theme of "the industrial revolution": steam-trains, iron bridges, steel works/furnaces, factory landscape, working people in factories, glowing metal, the mines, and so forth. An imaginative and technically accurate description naturally needs to precede each of these projects. Then the pupil can establish his/her own image fairly independently, whereby tightly painted areas should not be forgotten next to pictorial color interplay, with light and darkness playing a major role. In the ninth and tenth basic exercises an example is given how from a light-darkness setup a basis can be laid for this subject. A teacher constantly tries the basic colors and forms. It remains important to include the pupils in the best way of setting up a certain theme, otherwise the painting ends up too quickly in the "illustration" category, which tempts the pupils to work more with lines rather than out of the color area. "We have got to make it our habit again to use color perspective, not line-perspective, the sense of area, a sense of what is far off and what is close by, not via the line perspective, which always wants to magically create plastic forms on the area by means of trickery, but on the area via the color itself, which yields or comes closer intensively, not extensively."[20]

The pupils can try to process, in an assignment, the greatest possible contrast in color, a path of a light faded yellow to a deep dark purple-brown and a blue-like black. Steam, smoke and soot are well- suited to these types of themes. We could be inspired by the work of Turner. Between light and darkness, from whirling color movements the image of, for example, a steamship on the water in the setting sun is created. The assignments can be worked out subsequently in charcoal. Working out a theme in various ways and techniques will be covered in the next classes.

If a class is familiar with the veiling technique, the subjects mentioned above can also be painted in this technique. If this is not the case, it may be better to start with simpler assignments. In the drawing and painting lessons in eighth grade (usually given in double hours), it is important that wet-on-wet painting and veiling technique are alternated with working with pencil and charcoal. This is the teacher's way to accommodate the pupils' need for different activities.

* Basic exercises #8c and #8d for the teacher

These two assignments, very similar in format, are excellent exercises to give the subject of "the industrial revolution" form in

---

20. See Steiner's *Colour*, London: Rudolf Steiner Press, GA 291, twelve lectures, 2001.

color. They can also be done with the pupils. It should not be difficult to think of variants on the basis of the method described below. The first one could be titled "steam-train."

We take the paper before us standing up. In our head we split the paper into three vertical parts. We call this a "strip" for the sake of convenience. We start with Prussian blue. At the top of the first strip, top left, we start painting a strong blue reducing in strength downward to end up with a very weak blue at the bottom left.

Now we carry on with the middle strip. In this part too we paint a transitional strong Prussian blue to a very light blue, but the darker tints are at the bottom and decrease in strength upwardly. On the last strip, on the right, we repeat this transition and this one ends up looking like the first strip on the left of the sheet, dark at the top and light at the bottom. It is important to make sure that the separation between the strips is not too defined. The difference in color should be quite clear on the spot, but the line that is created as a separation need not be a tight straight boundary. From this light and darkness dynamic we now make a steam-train come towards us. From the darkness of the middle strip (bottom part) we paint the bumper, the rounded front of the boiler, the steam-pipe on top and behind this, the cabin. These details are already painted in the faded blue section of the middle strip. The light tints of the painting are middle top and left and right bottom, below the train. They suggest smoke and/or steam.

So as not to let the light run off the sheet, we close off these light spaces by painting dark blue along the edges of the paper. This gives the impression that in the top of the painting a puff of smoke comes from the chimney and in the bottom next to the train clouds of steam escape. After we have finished painting this, everything is carefully painted over with vermilion red. This changes the Prussian blue into indigo.

Where proportionally too much red is painted, appropriate red-brown tints are created. Finally a little yellow can be applied for accents. Practice shows that many pupils like to give this train two round lights. The paint can be removed from two spots and then painted in with yellow.

For the second assignment we take the sheet before us lying down. The subject now is "industrial area." Again we make an imaginary division of the sheet into three horizontal strips. We take the top strip first and we start at the top left and paint, in Prussian blue, a transition from dark to light up to the center (middle top) and from light to dark (to top right). We repeat this in reverse order for the middle strip, from light to dark up to the center and then lightening up towards the outside. The bottom strip is a repeat of the top strip. Again a strong light/dark color interplay on the paper.

In and with the dark blue in the center we now paint an industrial complex: factories, chimneys, roofs, buildings perhaps with windows, anything that fits in with this subject. At the top and bottom the light spots remain intact for the most part. Just as we did in the last assignment, we are going to close off these light spots with a dark blue. This suggests smoke clouds and plumes at the top of the landscape. By closing off the light at the bottom too, the painting becomes more threatening and more exciting. There is a strong temptation to let the factory be reflected in the bottom light spot. This makes the factory located on the water. This color is also painted "around" to the color indigo with vermilion red. Other colors can now be painted freely in one's own choice to further round off the theme.

Naturally the pupils can use these assignments to fully visualize their own ideas and fantasies. These two exercises can be done in an identical way with charcoal. It is exciting to do this in two subsequent sessions. The buildup of the work is the same and yet different results are produced.

2.11 Black and white drawing in sixth, seventh, and eighth grades

The study of light in sixth grade as part of the physics lessons should help to reproduce imaginative drawings, based on observation of light and shadow. A few exercises to explore the medium could be a proper beginning. Charcoal is preferred because of the many possibilities this medium offers, from light grey to very dark. The charcoal for the first few lessons can be home made! Charcoal is produced by taking moisture and volatile chemical substances from the wood by means of heating. The art of charcoal burning is to produce exactly the right degree of heat when burning hay and osiers to make thick and thin pieces of wood turn into charcoal and not burn to ashes. The exact preparation of charcoal requires a great deal of experience. Charcoal burning is an art in itself.

First of all within a circle with a six- to eight-meter diameter a post is hit into the ground. Following this, wooden trunks are placed around it with the thick/bottom side up. The farther the circle is filled up with trunks (to the outside), the shorter the wood the charcoal burner chooses. This gives the charcoal pile the shape of an arched dome. Subsequently the carefully built up woodpile needs to be covered up in the correct way, using earth and grass. To prevent this from ending up in the hollow of the charcoal pile and thus disrupting the charcoal burning process, the charcoal burner first carefully covers the pile with small thin pieces of wood, and on top of this he lays the grass sods and the black charcoal burner's soil. To make sure the fire has enough air and to help the smoke escape, he makes holes in the earth layer the diameter of a man's arm with a piece of wood.

Lighting is done at the top where the post sticks out of the pile. The osiers are around it. The charcoal burner has to continually make new openings to keep the fire burning, and he needs to close other holes. Because the transition from wood into charcoal goes hand in hand with a shrinking process, the charcoal burner has to climb the pile with the use of a ladder and stamp it well, so that the charcoal gives and collapses. After a week the wood has turned into charcoal. Then all holes are closed and the fire goes out. All that remains is to dig and sort out.

Transforming a white sheet into a grey one, with charcoal cloud- like effects, is a first assignment. The pupils can find lively ways to do this. The charcoal can be held at an angle so that a flat, small areas is created.

Alternatively, turn it on its side. Both ways promote working in areas. In this respect working with charcoal follows directly painting at the elementary school level. The pupils find it rather awkward to start with. Some are inclined to cover the sheet routinely with large strokes. This does not make a lively grey. The stripe-like areas give little room for further development. A careful "moving," letting the areas "grow," gives more open opportunities. The area eventually stands on its own. It finds peace. The skills which need to be developed are mainly in the searching for qualities in the grey-black field.

On the created silver-grey sheet several darker spaces can be made: darkness in misty surroundings, everything without any boundaries. This is established by subtle transitions and a gradual obscuring process. Steps 1 and 2 continue to be basic exercises for the next assignments.

If we carry on with this process the pupils can create boundaries between light and darkness, rounded curved boundaries as well as angular straight ones in all their variations, sharply edged obscured areas as well as white or grey "left open" spaces. The possibilities increase in view of the divergent results now becoming visible in class. A boundary is a separation between a lighter and a darker area. So with the pupils we talk about "bordering" as opposed to the overlapping / running into one another of different grey tones.

Within "bordered" areas the light and dark can be further varied. This causes the creation of all sort of free floating "objects" / forms. Subjects such as mountains, valleys, water and skies, trees, and so forth, can be developed from one's own imagination. This allows the pupils to practice concentration, balance, composition, and technical skills. Some will find only two or three shades of grey between black and white. Others may discover as many as five or six. This is very closely related to the degree of observation they are capable of and then processing those observations.

The darkening of the sheet can also be practiced in such a way that one or more "left open" light spaces are created in the center. One is easily inclined to determine the boundary alongside the form, moving with the form. When following this method the light space is not created by "leaving open," but by the striped movements along the "left open" area which have a line or circle character. To prevent this requires a certain measure of discipline on the pupils' behalf. When discussing the pupils' work in class the above mentioned quickly becomes clear.

When the pupils are relatively familiar with these first steps, which is usually at the end of sixth grade or the beginning of seventh grade, we can present them with new possibilities. Acquired charcoal drawing skills can be further applied through observation.

How is a closer observation of objects possible? By asking the question: "What do you see?" We take, for example, a big white globe and place this on a white sheet of paper with a light background. Daylight falls from the side on this setup: "a white globe." Now a concept of what has been observed is mentioned. The second question leads not to a description of what is represented, but to what is actually observed in the interplay between light and darkness. "Where is the light? Where is the dark?" and "Where are the transitions? The sharp contours between these two extremes?" We are asking after the different qualities of light and darkness. This sharpens the observation, makes it more mobile, more colorful, and it teaches the pupils to clarify and articulate their observations and to apply nuances. The pupils describe the lit-up curve contrasting with the dark backgrounds, transitions from right to left leading to the darkest part of the shadow side clearly distinguished from the lighter surroundings.

In this way we explore the form anew. We want to encourage keener observation by not asking after content, but by having the observation described precisely. We try to omit concepts as much as possible. The pupil discovers that shadow as well as light has the quality to evoke forms/shapes. The link between an object and the world around it is experienced and "seen" anew. The thirteen-, fourteen-year-old feels attracted to this new, down-to-earth point of view.

We look at a cone shape placed against a light background. Shadows are created by positioning a source of light obliquely above right or left. The pupils describe what they see. The next day this assignment is drawn, after first having recalled yesterday's observation. The pupils now use a very light grey to cover the paper (step 1). Now the dark is applied from the outside, leaving an open space for the cone shape. Each pupil draws the shadows on the object (by areas) according to his own observation. Everyone observes the object from his chosen point of view. In the second lesson the pupils check their own work by placing the setup in front of the class again.

We can repeat the foregoing with all sorts of other objects: cylinder, pyramid, bowl, sphere and cube. "Can we now draw the shadow which this object casts?"

The shadow having applied "on" the object, the created cast shadow is next. Quite a few aspects can be observed here and discovered. Is it long or short? Casting forward or backward? Round or pointed? What is the relationship between the shadow of the object and the area beside it? Which is darker? Does it have the same quality? Oh dear, the shadow of sphere and cube! How does the shadow carry on behind the object anyway? Many questions arise which can all be answered by careful [individual] observation, by walking around the object and observing it from many angles, high and low.

Towards the end of the seventh grade and the beginning of the eighth grade, we can make the assignments a little more complex. This also provides a great deal of differentiation within the lesson. After all, all these exercises can be done in parts. Now the object's shadow falls on a side/back wall. Or on a stair shape. The pupils could also draw more shapes, with shadows falling on other shadows: the shadow of a cone on that of a cube, and so forth. Rectangular box shapes can be drawn opened from various sides. The insides then become visible and also need to be included in the light-dark interplay. Before the pupils finish their work, it makes sense to view it from a distance and to discuss it. Each pupil can then see his own individual progress and can conclude from this what still needs to be done, a game of cause and consequence, of observation, trying and checking afterwards.

Each flicker of light has a cause. The observation is connected with thinking through doing—a start of the development of judgment. During all these exercises the pupils offer many of their own ideas. They try to further expand their own boundaries, building increasingly difficult assignments for themselves.

In this way the process of creative drawing from the imagination is analyzed and reflected. When the black has too fixed a form the pupils have to think of and execute gradual solutions. If, however everything remains too clouded and vague, then the work requires structure and form. The spatial effect of the drawings is considerable; perspective is created. The pupils look into space, around the objects. While drawing they search for a balance, for harmony between light and darkness. The eighth grade pupil senses the approaching darkness of loneliness, but also experiences the points of light in a slowly developing process of consciousness in which they learn to ask questions. Letting the pupils go through artistic processes is giving them a helping hand to guide them through the uncertain lessons of puberty.

2.12 Perspective and dissections in seventh and eighth grades

In seventh and eighth grades the pupils express the need to find out more about drawing, for example, other houses, landscapes, corridors and objects. The work done in the main lesson books or during the drawing lesson no longer suffices: "It doesn't look like it is supposed to at all," or "It's all at an angle, it just doesn't seem right." There is always a pupil in class who does know how certain lines and areas should be drawn to make it look "real." Someone taught him/her a few tricks, which he/she applies amongst the admiring glances of his/her fellow pupils.

How does the constructive element of perspective drawing fit in with the sequence of skills the pupils have acquired? The first front/ behind aspects we encountered in the fourth grade form-drawings, a conscious handling of bottom and top on the flat area in numerous

Celt and Longobard motifs. Geometric forms are drawn by hand, without compasses or rulers. In the same class and the next one color perspective is developed in the painting lesson: depth in the landscape through the effect of different color areas. Constructing geometric shapes with the help of compasses and ruler takes place in the geometry lessons in sixth and seventh grades. In the physics lessons the experiments with color, light and darkness are covered. The way the light falls and shadows work with different objects are observed and drawn in charcoal. All this culminates with a study of the skies, an orientation in space from the human perspective. Practicing perspective drawing then rests on this supportive layer.

One day the seventh grade pupils and their teacher go out the front door and take a short walk in the area surrounding the school. On a street with houses and trees on either side the teacher tells them to stop. "All of you, have a look at the end of the street. What can you see? Have a look at the trees, the cars parked alongside the pavement." The answers automatically come forward. The more distant, the smaller things are. "We'll keep this in mind for awhile, even though this is perfectly ordinary to us." Now the teacher chooses a spot with a wide view of the landscape. Questions and answers lead the pupils to an awareness that in the distance everything looks smaller. The walk is continued a few days later. One sunny day the pupils are sent out with a strong piece of cardboard, drawing paper and a pencil in hand. They find the same locations and try to make good sketches. Later on in class, they each choose one of their drawings and develop it further with colors, according to their own initial observation. After becoming a little more adept at sketching, the students can attempt inside areas, for example the long school corridor, maybe even the classroom. But this is more difficult, one is so close to things inside. The school yard and the garden, the ditch with the bridge nearby, everything is suitable for this assignment.

Now constructive directions can be given and practiced. Objects decreasing in size, lines and areas coming together, directly drawn from the surrounding—these form a good basis for the more abstract technical developing of the assignment with the aid of a ruler. Many children do not yet come to the idea of "vanishing points." Developmentally, they are not yet sufficiently experienced and therefore unable to consciously grasp the concept, for this concept is related to the emergence of the astral body. The stories of the voyages of discovery in seventh grade run parallel. Subjects from the main lesson or stories could also be used in painting, for example the foam on the waves behind the departing ships of Columbus. This is a way the "vanishing point" can become a manageable concept, although there are still pupils who will not "see" yet, and those are given the time and space to do so.

Not until eighth grade, when the second seven-year period is coming to a close, do we present fully perspective drawing. We draw a cube with another one beside it at the same height. The work of a pupil, who has drawn the second cube smaller becomes a lead-in to drawing a series of cubes of ever decreasing size, an awkward task. Drawing a cube with one edge to the front and a decreasing series of cubes behind it shows clearly that we are dealing with two vanishing points. They appear, sometimes on the sheet, but usually on the table next to the drawing paper. Now the class will really start moving, for they discover yet another peculiarity, an invisible line between the two vanishing points, which makes us look on top of the object or at it when we draw above or below this line. The cubes are piled up while painting. Then the third vanishing point comes up and impressive buildings are created as well as odd distortions.

Now we can draw the cube like an oblong space, open on one side. Doors and windows and preferably stairs are placed in it, and then the roof. This requires an insight into technique: halving the width of a house by drawing the diagonals of a wall. A straight line erected from the point of intersection and the oblique roof will appear as desired. The oddest constructions are now created with lots of imagination and / or very tightly technical, with straight and even curved lines (Roman curves).

In the eighth grade drawing lessons one way to begin can be by discussing and copying the construction of the perspective-device attributed to Dürer. A woodcut from *Dürer Education in Measuring with Compasses and Ruler,* pictures a device which can transfer three-dimensional objects onto a two-dimensional area. The draughtsman sits in front of his drawing, which is attached to a vertically-hinged frame which in turn is attached to a table on which the object, in this case a lute, is lying. When the draughtsman's helper turns the drawing sideways the artist looks along a thread, the loose end of which is held to a point on top of the lute. The thread goes through the frame to a point which the artist marks by stretching a horizontal and vertical thread. The thread to the lute is then released and the drawing is turned back to its original position, so that the artist can now record the indicated spot. The drawing is turned away once more and the line is held onto the lute from the next point. Marking takes place again, the drawing is returned to its original position, and the new point is recorded. This process is repeated many times. Slowly but surely the circumference of the lute is created out of the markings, in a correct perspective. This woodcut was printed in 1525 to portray, according to Dürer, a practical device for painters, goldsmiths, sculptors, stonemasons and joiners alike. He goes on to write that no one is compelled to use it, but he was convinced that those who would study it would carry on researching this device and discover much more than he could demonstrate.

This method of perspective drawing could be further developed by using a small window in the school, strung with horizontal and vertical threads. For many children this is a surprising new method compared to the earlier exercises. In addition drawings and paintings by various artists can be observed. "How did they manage to suggest depth?" When viewing Giotto, for example, we find many overlapping human figures. With Fra Angelica there is a structured space around Mary in *The Annunciation*. Finally, Escher tricks us all with his marvelous "distortions." Which eighth grade pupil would not want to know about the perpetually flowing waterfall or the stairways which cannot be made in practice but seem feasible in a drawing.

At home the children can apply themselves to making spy boxes. By drawing, painting, cutting, and sticking the pupils try to suggest as much depth as possible in their small shoe boxes. Light, shapes, windows, and color also play important parts in this experiment. Highways disappearing into tunnels with cars properly decreasing in size are created, or beautiful interiors, in which the furniture ingeniously suggests deep rooms, also imaginative landscapes with mountains, valleys, lakes and seas. Some pupils even use little mirrors, wool and beeswax to mislead the viewer.

Finally we have the description of a "cube-change" assignment. The largest possible cube with a forward edge and the top visible is drawn with the help of two vanishing points. On one of the vertices (say the upper right corner) a cube shape is "taken out." This "taken out" shape, however, turns up again on the left front at the top. It is as if someone pushed against the cube and slid a shape through the cube to the back. In principle this exercise can be done from all angles. Then a pupil discovers that it is also possible to deepen the middle of a plane which comes out again on the other side. By now giving each plane direction a certain grey tone or color the cube change becomes more obvious or "colored." All these exercises plus many more enable the children to skillfully construct drawings in their main lesson books.

The development of perspective drawing runs parallel with drawing "dissections" from seventh grade onward. These exercises link up with black and white drawing in sixth grade. Steiner described in his second lecture on the curriculum "that the technical [aspect] now needs to be joined with beauty."[21] He proposed the following as an example in seventh grade: "Here is a cylinder cut in two by a wooden beam. The beam needs to cut through the cylinder. You must show what type of section is created in the cylinder on the spot where the beam goes in and comes out. This must be imparted to the children. The children should learn what happens when bodies or planes dissect each other, so that they know the difference between a stove pipe going straight through the ceiling or at an angle, creating an ellipse."

It is up to the teacher to think of many other assignments in seventh and eighth grades using these examples: round poles cutting through square beams and vice versa, round poles dissecting each other from various angles, handles and spouts on pots and jars, chimneys and dormer windows on houses, balconies and conservatories on buildings. When pupils in seventh and eighth grades have acquired a taste for this, they themselves come up with divergent examples. When thirteen-, fourteen-, and fifteen-year-olds make this connection between technique and beauty it can have an enormous effect.

21. See Steiner: *Practical Advice for Teachers*, third and fourth lectures, London: Rudolf Steiner Press, 1976.

3. High School

3.1 Introduction

Around the fourteenth year (the end of eighth grade) the adolescent pupil becomes caught up in physical and emotional changes related to what Steiner calls "earth ripeness." This development is first heralded in sixth and seventh grades, for example, in the artistic work. The lessons of imagination (seven to fourteen years) comes to an end. The wealth of images disappears. Individual judgment is developing in fits and spurts. New feelings catch the old certainties by surprise. The astral or perception body is awakened. These changes are expressed differently in girls than in boys. The differences in the way they experience things is considerable. Extreme feelings of loneliness and insecurity alternate with recklessness and unbridled exuberance. A totally different attitude from the teacher is called for now. The trusted, often revered class teacher is no longer the obvious leader. A high school teacher should now, first and foremost, be a human being and an expert. At best he/she will become a friend. The same goes for the drawing and painting teacher. His/her expertise, together with a sense of humor, will create the necessary atmosphere in which each pupil can contribute positively.

For a curriculum tuned into the psychology of the developmental stages Steiner recommends dropping work with color in adolescence (particularly in ninth grade), so that black and white art, in itself already a pertinent image for the experiences of the adolescent, can come to the fore completely. There are plenty of examples in the history of art of suitable and varied techniques using black and white. The young secondary school pupil strongly experiences these extremes between light and dark. Between him/herself and the world of objects the animation/inspiration of childhood falls away. In the world around, in matter, death looks upon him. Opposite this dead chill he experiences the unknown, uncontrolled life within himself.

By using black and white art we try to understand the workings of the light. The light animates things in the world, gives them "color," even though we are working with black and white. In light and color the laws of the cosmos are revealed, an aid to security. Finally, light also makes beauty visible, the beauty one experiences and which "consequently" exists. As testimony from a higher world, art is one of the few "things" in which you can keep on believing as an adolescent.

The themes for the assignments are kept simple, but considerable attention is given to development and finish. In the first instance emphasis is on nuances of the light in a bird's eye view of an interior space. In the second, renewed experience and exploration of the world of color, as well as technique, must be focal points.

The teacher will have a different way of working with each class, because each group has a different character. When choosing an assignment, technical perfection or a thematic program is not his objective, rather the development stage in which the group finds itself and the special interests which emanate from this. Art is a means to express the invisible, the unspeakable. For those practicing this expression, it is of particular value to compare their own work with that of others or to make comparisons between simultaneous assignments, similar themes and "metamorphic" works. Steiner suggested the following examples: sunrise and sunset, trees in the sun and trees in the storm. Thus one theme changes into another: Summer turns into autumn in the next project, and so forth.

Discussing before and after a project is a subtle matter also at secondary level. Just enough should be said to spark enthusiasm. The art itself (together with known works of art) needs to be looked at critically. A balance has to be struck. The material that has preceded as introduction and assignment to the creation of a piece of work is extremely important when "judging," the "viewing" or exhibiting the work. Work by the pupils should never really be judged or exhibited solo or without accompanying explanation, although the tendency to do so at secondary school is considerable. The teacher can see to it that pupils both sign, date or number the work, and make mention of the assignment or theme.

The practicing aspect of all the artistic work is the first consideration of the lessons. In this way, the work modestly detaches itself from "grand art," but the actual theme is the same: creating an image from the connection between inner and outer concepts. Through this process the pupils experience what it is like to be in the shoes of the Impressionists or Expressionists. While doing, the pupils also experience the difference between inspiration and assignment or, in other words, the moment between imagination and necessity, material-wise, the game, human freedom. Then with this experience he can become mildly aware of the creative process referred to in Schiller's remarkable book *Letters about the Aesthetic Education of Mankind* [*Briefe über die aesthetische Erziehung der Menschen*].

In all classes particular attention is given to composition and color detail. The teacher will point out the possibilities for expressing more than what is photographically, academically and technically correct. Conversely, he will continue to balance imagination with visible reality or the reality of the assignment. In twelfth grade, after having investigated all forms of draftsmanship throughout history up to the shading in our time, free drawing of stove, plant, animal and people can be taken up again, for example, in a homemade self-bound sketch book.

Steiner does not give any indications with regards to animal painting at the secondary level, as he does for painting plants. (see eleventh grade curriculum) When drawing animals, sketching according to nature is the best way to capture the character.

In this way the secondary school pupils' skills grow in a number of techniques in well-considered assignments. Not all techniques can be practiced at school. Experience shows us that the technical skills, built up over so many years (e.g., use of watercolor) enable the pupils' imaginations, which are carefully and gradually released after puberty, to gain form, color, and context.

Freedom to choose one's own assignment does not usually lead to a satisfactory result (even with a twelfth grade pupil): Properly structured assignments, individually tailored, make an appeal to the pupil and help form a connection to other themes in the subject matter. Creating from nothing requires considerable application of the will. The assignment to make, for example, a picture book for a toddler about a certain story directs the imagination and provides enthusiasm, even though it limits the size and target group. In this way the pupil experiences the dilemma of the artist between assignment and inspiration, question and answer, and his freedom in between those. It is the specific task of the high school art teacher to offer the pupils experiences that help boost self confidence.

The indications Steiner gave for working at the secondary school level are as many as the questions that were asked at the time which he could answer. Even now we can only find the answers if we know how to ask the questions in practice in sympathy with the pupils. By properly taking note of the few indications given by Steiner and by understanding how this still is linked to the psychology of the secondary school pupil, today's teacher will find contemporary and personal variations for the assignments within the curriculum. Hence many didactic experiences have been skipped here and references to Steiner's suggestions only appear only now and then.

The curriculum for the high school as described here also includes basic exercises as lesson preparation for content and technical aspects.

3.2 Painting in the ninth grade

The art teacher is subject teacher in ninth grade. His professional skill, discipline, authority and humor help the fourteen- to fifteen-year-old pupils struggle through the method and process prescribed.

* Basic exercise #9 for the teacher

We observe for awhile what light "does," shining through a little shutter in a shoe box. For example, it "falls" on the bottom and "colors" the walls in various tints of grey. All this we draw on a large scale piece of paper with charcoal, starting with the grey tones on the wall areas, without sketching lines around the forms of the areas. We leave an open space for the window. The darkest area (where is that?) is applied strongly in black, and between this black and the white, as many grey tones as possible appear, bordered and running from dark to light and vice versa.

On the enlarged format the structure of the areas should not dominate the working of the light. So "shading it grey" with a steady, even hand until the areas have settled down and the boundaries are sharp is recommended. For many a pupil this is a struggle at first. But as soon as all the white has disappeared from the paper (except for the window) the interior space starts to tell a story making all the monotonous work worthwhile.

Dürer as a source of inspiration for black and white drawing

Mastering the materials is of crucial importance to pedagogy during puberty. Hard work and investigation are needed. Such an investigative and conquering attitude makes artists like Dürer into Renaissance men. This has a special effect on the ninth grade pupil (and the secondary school pupil in general). Once captivated by the teacher's introduction of Dürer's fascinating themes and technique, the pupils try to follow and comprehend the master. As an introduction Dürer's biography could be told or a description given of the times in which he lived. With the help of *Writing Hieronymus*, the significance of physical and spiritual light (around the head of a saint) can be examined. In *Melancholia* we find an image in which mystical wisdom is depicted. We can explore the interaction of light with darkness. We are not concerned with analyzing symbolism in the engraving, but pupils' observations and questions should be encouraged.

So the first work in ninth grade could be exploring *Melancholia* with eye and hand, not by means of sketching or boundary lines, but by indicating the shadows with charcoal. Gradually the mysterious representation shows up: the heavy angel figure, the small chubby angel, the polyhedron, the globe, the dog, the light in the distance, and so forth. Enlarging the format is an excellent exercise. This enlargement can be dealt with technically at first for the whole class. The pupils work from a copy of true proportions, possibly with the support of a blackboard drawing by the teacher. "Where does the light come from?" we ask when the drawing is finished, and the observations become experience. The aim is not just the composition, but the light on and around the things with its rules and pictorial character.

Alternatively we could precede the study of Dürer's engravings with reconstructing black and white drawing starting with the simplest aspects, as follows. With graphite or charcoal (Siberian chalk could also be used) a black area is applied from the top left fading downward (sticking to the left) with a random boundary (on the right). Subsequently the right hand side of the sheet is drawn from the top very lightly down to the bottom black in all transitions of grey. A great deal of attention is paid to the meeting of the two areas. A vertical black or white line should not be created. The work is continually observed from a distance to be able to correct it oneself. The same exercises can be done with the horizontal or other boundaries.

We start a second drawing at the top again with black, across the entire width of the paper. In this area which gradually gets lighter going down, we leave a round space. This "left open" circle is "colored" in, starting from the top with the lightest grey up to black. The actual "rounding" of the circle as well as going through all the grey tones is corrected by the pupils themselves as soon as they view their work from a distance.

For a next exercise we take a simple white object on which shadow and light are easily noticed, a white ball or a roll of toilet paper. The surrounding area is made grey. The space for the object is left open. To be able to see the object a little from the top and to see the shadow properly in the background and foreground, one should not be too far away and slightly higher than the subject. Not only should the object be white, but so should the background and the area underneath. A sheet of drawing paper behind and one underneath the object work very well. The white paper shows extremely delicate grey tones. With this setup we make an interesting interim exercise. White paper is ideal for observation of delicate light-shadow nuances. A piece of paper folded open or slightly crumpled up can be copied with fine drawing equipment, e.g., graphite. This requires a great deal of concentration from the ninth grade pupil, but as soon as half of it is done, the visible part kindles the enthusiasm and the improved skill allows the white to appear on white with few brush strokes. It is an assignment for one lesson. Working on it a second time is impossible, because the slightest change in light alters everything. And a crumpled piece of paper is hard to reproduce accurately after it has been cleared away.

Now we take a more difficult object from one of Dürer's engravings: the sphere, the bell, the key, the skull. Depending on the length of the lesson, this is an assignment for at least two classes, so that one can realize a distance from the work in between time. Again, there are two ways of working. The first one: We have the object before us and we copy it. The second one: We take Dürer's engraving, observe closely how he has drawn the object, and reproduce it on a larger scale. Dürer uses lines. We can either follow these precisely or with a different approach, for example, with the flat area of the charcoal, we can achieve the same grey tones from the alternating black and white shades in the engraving. It is best, by the way, to use the same method as described above, for example, shading the background with grey leaving a space open for the object. So, we draw the surroundings, in other words the light in which the object sits. Then we reproduce what we see as a shadow on the object (the object becomes spatial). And finally this spatial object casts a shadow in its surroundings (it removes the light). This shadow is usually the darkest and should be reproduced in the proper strength to connect object and space together.

The size of the paper we work on and the thickness of the drawing equipment should be compatible. The paper should not be too thin, just in case one goes "through" it. A large format has an activating effect and prevents rigidity. Maintaining a white edge around the paper has technical and pedagogical advantages: The sheet can be steadied (with a clean hand) and the straight edge is left open by gauging the boundaries with the drawing hand. So we should not first draw lines to keep the white edge free, but rather create the border during the shading process.

After working so intensively on the exterior of things we can now look at the interior space, for example *Hieronymus Writing in His Cell*, captured atmospherically by Dürer. To be able to observe the working of the light within a space in a simple way we can make use of an available pin hole box. A spy hole and one window are sufficient. This helps bring inner representation and outer observations closer together. One can also darken the classroom space except for one area where light comes in and draw this. Other spaces with, for example, a door ajar, light falling on one single table or one's own empty room also provide the opportunity to reproduce on paper the extreme tension between light and dark. A space can now be drawn at the outset like the one in which Hieronymus is depicted, but empty.

Following this exercise the Dürer engraving can now be roughly reproduced in a large format. In this assignment we are concerned with the relationship between light and dark, not with how each individual thing has been drawn. Here again we subordinate the line drawing to the "workings of areas." On the blackboard or on a large white piece of paper the teacher can give a broad outline of the proportions. The pupils can follow along and start the light-dark work in their own individual ways. Working in "squares" should be avoided. In the earlier part of the assignment we drew the room as an empty space, now similarly we can work by leaving open spaces for the objects and the Hieronymus figure (including the light around his head). Alternatively we can start with the image elements or work horizontally from top to bottom.

After a little while the work of a number of pupils is viewed jointly. The teacher can point out the different ways of working. When discussing the work we are better off not showing too much, but with the help of some examples clarify some "points of attention." Such points of attention are:

- evenly worked areas, so that the eye can go around things and can be carried along in the space;
- the sharpness of the area boundaries making forms visible;
- the proportions and the invisible connecting lines throughout the drawing.

Taking note of Steiner's recommendations to "develop the technical in an artistic way," we can, in ninth grade, place all sorts of constructions, objects or spaces in black and white, light-darkness, while we strongly emphasize the aesthetic. It is obvious that we are not concerned here with something external, but with bringing the lifeless empty world to life again by means of the light.

In this year's course craft and technique take up important positions in several subjects. Learning printing techniques, such as etching and linoleum block printing, connect with the need of the fourteen- to fifteen-year old to become acquainted with subject disciplines. The equipment has its demands. From these the technique grows, which the pupil can learn to manage. Work must be done in stages. The stress is not experimentation or long term design at this age. If such a printing technique is employed then, we should stick initially to simple black and white themes in which the aspects of light and dark are covered in just such a way as in drawing. Afterwards a report of the work process could be written. There should be sufficient work for each pupil (especially in the ninth grade). Working with groups (e.g., two half classes) provides the teacher with more opportunities for advising and encouraging. The great urge of the ninth grade pupil to perform is controlled by the gradual, step by step technique. Simple, carefully chosen and monitored themes help the pupils understand quicker the working of the light. A single example of the work from previous years or higher classes and the meeting with Dürer's "masterwork" usually suffice as sources of inspiration.

Steiner recommends the use of Dürer's engraving as suitable for the fourteen- to sixteen-year old. If work has already been done on this in eighth grade, perhaps through the guidance of an elementary school colleague, then it is necessary to know what has been done and how. One can then elaborate or vary to fit in with the particular class of ninth grade pupils.

Drawing and painting in connection with art history

The Waldorf curriculum is a totality, not only vertically throughout the years of learning, but also horizontally in the connections between the various subjects. Thus art history takes up a central position in ninth grade being linked to drawing, painting and clay modeling. The strong physical and emotional changes taking place within the young person have unsettled the relationship with him/herself and the world, hence the considerable importance of becoming acquainted with ideals such as those of Egyptian and Greek sculpture. Through the indelible power of beauty unity becomes apparent in a world which is falling apart around the adolescent person. The art history lessons (lasting four to six weeks) facilitates this intensive encounter with the essence of beauty. By recreating ancient works of art the pupil grows closer to them. Visits to museums, good slides and/or copies, photographs or clear prints, but above all carefully drawn blackboard drawings by the teacher can help accomplish this "closeness." It is, however, mainly about the way the teacher motivates the pupils to experience awe during the drawing process for what humanity has achieved by the hand of the artist in the works of art under discussion. Drawing, clay modeling or painting work should reflect the characteristics of an era.

When the pupils are executing drawing or painting assignments (e.g., in the main lesson books), the teacher will attach great value to the way light-dark have been expressed, especially in the reproduction of sculptures. In painting the colors can be adjusted. The correct representation of proportions and perspective is also appropriately given attention at this age, for example, to avoid drawings with columns that are too thin or too short. Making some well worked out drawings can capture the essence of an era much better than viewing many words or slides. The blackboard drawings and the printed material the pupils work with must serve as examples, in other words, the print should reflect the lines of the original. (Many photocopiers give poor quality copies, and, furthermore, working with photocopiers promotes a throw-away attitude.) When such working materials are placed in a transparent folder/sleeve or in a cardboard folder, they will remain, hopefully, treasured possessions for years to come.

In the blackboard drawings the teacher can aim specifically to reproduce the atmosphere of the image, beside good use of perspective. This aim can be achieved by working amply with color, by using color perspective. One can also use large black and white examples to encourage independent work. They will remain as beacons, hopefully, in their memories.

Basic exercise #10 for the teacher

This exercise aims to show how to transform the black and white work of the basic exercise 9 freely into color. This "transforming to color" can be freely encouraged; working systematically is not the idea here. Steiner recommends Dürer's black and white art as a basis for transforming into color. Here we have simplified the image content. In the space only the light works. With this light we leave open spaces, and a systematic transformation remains initially vague. That is why it lends itself to be wetted again (to work on another time or to be "veiled" on stretched paper.[22]

On a loose sheet one starts working as follows. The dry painting is turned over on a dry table and the back of the sheet dabbed with a wet sponge, so that the complete sheet absorbs the water (do not overdo it). Then the paper is turned over with the working side showing (pick it up carefully with two hands at the corners), smoothed either while painting or dabbing with a small sponge or clean cloth, to turn the surface "matt." The layers that now follow are a confirmation of the forms and colors already present. They are applied in a more "veiling" way, that is, not too much wet on the brush and positioned in designated areas.

Basic exercise #11 for the teacher

On a dry (previously wet) stretched watercolor paper we paint initially with one color. The stretching of the paper and the preparation of the paint and other initial steps have been described in sixth grade. In this basic exercise we are concerned with refining the technique and experiencing the tension between center color and periphery color. Basically one can start with any color and any form of veiling. With "form of veiling" we mean the way the brush

---

22. See descriptions in the sections on the sixth and tenth grades.

is manipulated on paper. This can vary a great deal: large rectilinear bordered areas, round, straight and round, medium sized and small areas. When painting with diluted paint it is important that the paper is able to soak up all the water used. So the motto is: Start as dry as possible. To apply another layer to this foundation one brush stroke should suffice. When going over the first brush stroke with a second one, the paint of the first layer will dissolve and is easily removed; what is left is a bare patch. For the purpose of veiling the watercolor paint should be thinly prepared.

So, if the choice for the initial color is blue, Prussian blue (very thinly prepared), for example, we paint the blue color all around in large straight/curved areas. The stronger the color—we put the painting at a distance and view it—the clearer we see the effect of the rosa-red contrasting color in the white part left open. Independently of this we choose a color to paint the inner area. So now we concentrate on placing (at least in some spots) the Prussian blue and, for example, an orange.

Where they overlap (accidentally or purposely) a brown-like dark tone is created. It is very difficult to paint next to the first painted form. If it is allowed to dry well in the meantime, the running [of colors] is not a problem (unless the paint is not thin enough).

When we have balanced inside and outside color by means of the proper dilution of paint, the number of layers, and the color proportion on the sheet, we are ready for the next step. With the exception of one or two sections (which remain blue and orange) we change the Prussian blue by painting, for example, yellow over it (again veiling in several layers). Now, in our example orange stands in predominantly green. Some of the initial color of orange can be preserved, when part of it is painted over with violet. The violet is obtained by mixing a sufficient quantity of paint (carmine

+ ultramarine) on the palette or in a mixing tray. A completely new, perhaps unsatisfactory, color harmony is created. The remaining orange and the clear Prussian blue are preserved as initial colors somewhere in the painting and the rest is changed in the subsequent layers. This is how deeper tints of black-brown are created until all the green and all the violet are changed. The second contrast, violet-green, consequently changes into red-brown, or blue-green, and the initial colors make for a harmonious whole.

While experimenting, one gains a lot of experience in the creation of color and color drama. Because of the step by step technique and the restriction of choices, one also learns about the rules and restrictions of certain color harmonies. (see Chapter 6.1) A monotone combination is essentially different from a characteristic or a harmonious one. It makes sense for us to become aware of this. The next question is: Which color can lighten up or tone down?

Because the veiling requires a great deal of drying (waiting) time, but also because comparison makes the specifics visible, we can work on three separate pieces in turn. We start all three with the same color combination, we change with two different colors (different in all three projects) and end with the two initial colors. Compare the paintings and try to typify the differences and describe them in the formulation of a title.

3.3 Painting in the tenth grade
Movement and order in black and white and color

The tenth grade pupil can, once he has a feel for imaginative studies, begin to work to create tension and drama in black and white as well as color studies. For example the tension and drama in a Rembrandt painting by removing the light, this is what the tenth grade pupil can now learn to work with. Trees, landscapes, people, objects and architectural forms can be silhouetted or a pupil's own schoolbag or shoe will be seen in a new light. Emphasis is on light/dark contrast.

The tenth grade pupil clearly has more staying power than the pupil in ninth grade and is capable of working on a project for longer and more concentrated lessons. On the basis of exercises in previous classes he/she is capable of technical refinement. If Dürer's work was not discussed in ninth grade, then make sure it is in the tenth grade. The theme of the inspired clergyman in *Hieronymus Writing in His Cell* and of the melancholy, brooding angel in *Melancholia* form images of the human on his way to self-awareness. Steiner points out the importance of introducing the adolescent pupil to these images. The eagerness with which the pupils work on these themes shows how accurate Steiner's indication is. As described for ninth grade we are not concerned with copying Dürer's work, but with studying light/darkness.

If the pupils are sufficiently familiar with an image as a whole, it can be "freely" transformed into color. This exercise can also be started as early as eighth grade,[23] in the light of previous coverage of the Renaissance. In tenth grade we are becoming more aware of the Baroque (Rembrandt). Even though Steiner recommended transforming Dürer's black and white work into a color fantasy, it is not an easy task. The practiced painter quickly experiences the following: The laws of the meeting of yellow (light) and blue (dark) in green on the one side or red-purple (purple) on the other are not systematically followed.

---

23. See Steiner's *Conferences with the Teachers of the Waldorf School in Stuttgart,* February 5, 1924, Forest Row, England: Steiner Schools Fellowship Publications, 1989.

Dürer's work contains a reflection of matter and atmosphere in black and white. The pupil has become familiar with this in the course of his work in ninth grade, and the colors have had a year's rest. In order to get back to color again it is best to start with wet-on-wet at the beginning of a lessons. So we jump in at the deep end straight away. For example *Hieronymus Writing in His Cell* is painted "freely." What it means to paint "freely" the pupils will only notice when viewing the first results. A class discussion about the theme, about the atmosphere in the room and about Hieronymus, about his work, can help the pupils make their personal color choices. Also pointing out that the original engraving should be remembered rather than constantly checked, helps the pupils in loosening themselves from the plastic details and in transforming the entirety and the most important elements first into color. The work usually lends itself to be wetted again. The painting is placed upside down on a dry table or board and a wet sponge is carefully wiped over the back of the painting. The paper soaks up the water, it is turned over and flattened while painting. One can also dab it carefully with a clean cloth. Eighty gram paper is best for this purpose; this is also used at primary school level, because of its strength.

Apart from transforming black and white, the renewed meeting with the world of color takes place via the wet-on-wet painting. Here are some examples:

1. Red, blue and yellow, each coming from one side, meet in the center. There the three colors stand next to each other, not touching. Blue is painted over the large red area. Similarly we paint red over yellow and yellow over blue. The outside part of the purple we paint over with yellow, the green with red and the orange with blue, so that brown tints are created.

2. A red area in the green: The red should be vibrant in the green. Blacks are created, here and there red pushes through the green. Harmony in color and form are sought. All characteristic color combinations can be a starting point.

3. Purple and orange stand together in the colors least used: blue and yellow. Painting is continued until a balance is achieved. (see Chapter 4.1)

4. With indigo, vermilion and Prussian blue we create a black on paper! Golden yellow is added, brown is created, mixed tints are made with golden yellow and yellow. This is an intensive exploration with earth colors. The light remains in it.

5. At the top of the paper, white. At the bottom, black running very thinly into Prussian blue via indigo and ultramarine. The white is preserved. Around the white, light yellow radiating the Prussian blue and green is created.

6. Make as many areas of different colors creating strong boundaries. Colors can be created on the paper through mixing, but also with the help of the mixing tray. The pupils could also swap amongst each other. When all the colors stand next to each other, separated, hard, we paint over all or part of them with equal colors. "Obscuring" or "illumining" is being done. This part of the process is suitable for working out further on "re-wetted" paper in a subsequent lesson.

It is important for the pupils to have ample opportunity to gain the necessary experience for the veiling technique. This is why we start assignments using this technique as soon as possible. See also basic exercise 11 for the teacher.

Two sheets of painting paper are stretched (for a more complete description see discussion on sixth grade). On one sheet work is done in large veiling areas, on the other sheet with small rhythmic areas of different sizes. On one sheet we place a blue area opposite a yellow area. Moving on a bit we then paint some layers on top of each other in the same colors. Yellow overlaps yellow, blue overlaps blue. On the one side we let the green come about between the blue and the yellow by painting Prussian blue over yellow or yellow over blue. On the other side we paint red as the linking color between yellow and blue by painting vermilion over the yellow and carmine over the ultramarine blue. The vermilion and the carmine overlap. White can remain in the middle (but not too much). On the outer edges the complementary color can be painted in any color, so that black tints are created: green on top of red, orange on top of blue, violet on top of yellow, and red on top of green, and so forth. A crystalline image is created.

On the other sheet a foundation is painted in small areas from top to bottom, from yellow to orange to red through purple to blue indigo. In the middle of the sheet (vertically) these colors are "confirmed;" by that I mean the color ladder is intensified by the application of several layers. Left and right each color fans out and many mixed colors are created up to the color black. It is important to prevent "pointillism" or a patchy effect caused by too much wetness. Care and clarity are our aims, so that the colors start to radiate in the bordering grey. Examples from previous years, the pupils' own work or that of known artists can show how light and color strength can be achieved with the veiling watercolor technique. This second painting will remain a mood painting or become a landscape.

Each pupil has a palette with available dry watercolors or resealable jars containing slightly diluted paint. To dilute for veiling small mixing bowls can be used. Each pupil also has two or three rinsing jars (red, blue, yellow), broad and narrow brushes, and a cloth to remove superfluous paint or to dry a wet brush. In addition to the how and why of water control when veiling, during each lesson we teach the pupils to correct mistakes. With this control, the pupils can now achieve what they want to in the field of mixing or "making" colors. When veiling, the board can be held at a slight angle, so too much water is obvious and can be corrected. The pupils need to find their own work postures. Working on an easel promotes the viewing of the work at a distance.

Working on "veiled" painting requires a certain order. Each layer needs to dry properly before further work can be done. The sheet can be worked on several times per lesson, providing it dries well. We can use a drying cupboard (if it does not dry well by itself). The painting boards can be placed vertically inside it. The ventilator heater is placed under it. A lesson program in which veiling and wet-on-wet alternate is possible. During these veiling exercises, the middle section of the lesson, for example, can be used for wet-on-wet color exercises.

When the first veiling paintings are completed, painting paper is stretched again onto the boards for the next projects. There are many possibilities to set up a further exploration of color. The most important thing is that imagination itself, supported by a number of preliminary exercises and explorations, moves the brush and chooses color.

Initially one can—helped by the radiating effect of the veiling technique when working with larger areas—link up with the mineralogy lessons and paint crystals or the illumining inner world. Themes from cultural history can also be given shape in color and form, for example Atlantis. Conversely one can also look for perceptions in color dramatics in color exercises without representation. The colors themselves and brush control can easily become themes themselves. There is also the possibility of arriving at a color fantasy, starting from a black and white example, like Dürer's *Melancholia*. The composition of the master and the wealth of the image content with this particular engraving are sources of stability and inspiration for the young secondary school pupil. They can achieve some remarkable results when working on a large format. Some pupils do not shrink from reproducing the engraving of *Knight, Death and Devil* in color. As always these exercises are all about progress in the critical use of color, not simply copying. Finally doing two paintings on the same theme is very useful at this age. Here are some examples:

sunrise	-	sunset (see Chapter 6.2)
night	-	day
sunlight	-	moonlight
summer	-	winter
storm	-	calm
before battle	-	after battle

* Basic exercise #12 for the teacher
The root, leaf, flower, and fruit process in the plant is reproduced on one or several sheets. These paintings can be done both wet-on-wet and in the veiling technique. Hint: The project must be "done."

1. The root process: crystalline, cool, star-like left open spaces in a dark, warm environment.
2. The leaf process: blue and yellow coming together in green. Rhythmically repeating forms. Red (carmine) permeates all the plant green!

3. The flower or budding process: Light and airily painted carmine red and yellow (at the top) link up with blue at the bottom of the sheet (green is created). The connection with the insect world (e.g., bees or butterflies) we find by accentuating butterfly-like shapes together with flowers with specifically light yellow and rose.
4. The seeding process: The seed is inclined towards the earth. Each seed becomes an island of warm light (rounded shapes) in a cool environment.

When these four paintings are shown to a colleague who teaches biology in eleventh grade and is asked for comments, some interesting feedback is given. Question: How do we paint the process from 4 to 1? Together with this exercise one can study the *Urpflanze* watercolor by Steiner.

* Basic exercise #13 for the teacher

Next, this can yield another four exercises for the teacher, when the growth process, as described in the 12th basic exercise is rendered in the black and white shading technique. A description of shading can be found in eleventh grade.

1. The dark closes in the light that shines through the darkness.
2. Watery, rhythmically repeating forms are created in the meeting of light and dark.
3. In an environment of light, the dark hardly condenses; in some center points it contracts in a star-like fashion. This is where an open space is left for structured light.
4. The light penetrates the dark. The dark encloses the light shining within itself.

These last two basic exercises are a good preparation for eleventh grade.

3.4 Painting in the eleventh grade

Painting trees and plants in moods. The impression and the expression

In the sixteenth to seventeenth year of life we see the young people create large spaces around themselves; childlike qualities are discarded; they distinguish themselves more clearly from others; their own emotional world is more marked; love is experienced for the first time.

In the Waldorf curriculum during this time, biology, including botany, takes on a central position. The plant's essence shows us an image of the soul giving itself away in a characteristic gesture. Religious elements are important building blocks for the young person at this stage. The Parsifal main lesson in the literature curriculum not only answers many questions, but also helps to ask essential questions, especially those questions about one's own inner world, questions which are now becoming important in the artistic process. Steiner gives the example of painting a tree in eleventh grade. He recommends the "pictorial" way, not to take the green and the leaves as a starting point, but to approach the tree as if surrounded and imbued by light, to build up the image from color areas. Examples of Impressionists and Expressionists alike, who worked so much with the outer and inner "impression" of the natural phenomena, can also help define "art," how color and area are first and foremost the painter's media. What was done in fifth grade in a playful manner is repeated, but from a new awareness.

We take a further step by painting the same tree in different light conditions. The time of year could be different, the weather could vary. By comparing paintings we can begin to understand color and seek a connection with our inner being. After a first wet-on-wet painting of "the tree in light," we can divide a big stretched sheet in two or four to paint two or four seasons. We can discuss the nuances of color with the pupils. For the rest we live up to the idea of "pictorial," thus preventing "fine-writing." We should pay attention to the presence of red in the plant green. Plant green without red remains cold, mineral-like. This concept can give rise to some wet-on-wet paintings with different (flowering) plants, for example daffodils, poppies, lupine, roses, or types of trees. The teacher describes the plant in such as way that an inner image can be created. The comparative description and the expressing of an image, for example the daffodil "heralding spring with trumpet sounds," can be discussed with the class one or two lessons prior to the work being done. The plant or flower can also be observed in a previous lesson. Working with a carmine pink foundation is the best way to create the plant green from the various colors yellow and blue. After some encouragement the pupils apply the extra white-yellow, painted over the plant at the final stage (as indicated by Steiner in the color lectures), and they can see how the yellow with its connecting quality helps the light pervade the plant.

Beside these wet-on-wet paintings, we can work on spring or autumn flowers on stretched paper. This can perhaps be done on a large format. One can also take the lily and the rose, a special duo, and paint both. In this case the lily is more the spring flower with fresh juicy green and the rose the darker with warm red-like shoots.

The idea of "each pupil painting his own plant" requires a great deal of empathy on the teacher's behalf, but with proper long term preparation, and the pupil actively working on his rendering of the plant, this can yield very personal and intensely experienced results. It is important for the eleventh grade pupil to feel a certain measure of freedom in his/her own working pace. The pupil's own interests and contributions are given ample attention. A good variety of veiling and wet-on-wet prevents sinking into a complacent green. Most pupils no longer have problems with the technique. Some even show the marks of mastery. Going deeper into the work of the Impressionists and Expressionists (flowers by Nolde, for example) and into the inner attitude of the artist can strengthen the eleventh grade pupil in his/her attitude to work. The assignment "sunrise and sunset" (always inspiring), can also give the pupils the chance to produce deeper contrasting colors in their work.

Pupils (sometimes groups in class) who are battling with a considerable degree of doubt as to their own abilities, can be encouraged by using color in a pictorial way from black and white works by artists such as Rembrandt, Cezanne, and Van Gogh.

Various drawing techniques; shading. Drawing plants, animals and people
The moment has arrived in eleventh grade for both drawing and painting to lead/usher the pupils into the realm of modern art, for example, art in the beginning of the twentieth century. In music history terms such as "Apollonian" and "Dionysian" are now discussed, which give the pupil the growing realization of the two poles which have their point of application within people themselves and which cause our expressions to be "marked" or "colored." We encounter these extremes in drawing as well. The entire range of possibilities is practiced, from line-drawing to light-dark shading of areas, between observation and imagination.

Shading takes up a special place here. This technique enables us to render directly the spiritual effect of the light in the image. Shading can be covered in the eleventh grade, introduced by a study of draftsmanship through the centuries. The works of Dürer and

Rembrandt and others as forerunners can be taken up once again. By copying and enlarging we study the technique of the masters. Differences in emphasis in their methods become obvious. We can study the development through artists such as Van Gogh and Picasso.

When, subsequently, the pupils draw each other in all sorts of poses, they are not simply copying, but hopefully strengthening their own expressions through the conscious varying of the thickness of lines, rhythm in the shapes, structure in the areas, light and darkness proportions and so on. Shading requires a great deal of "I" activity, difficult for the pupil to summon. But exactly what is shading?

We place diagonal lines running right to left. This gives the light space on the paper. In that space hidden processes become visible. Because of the character of the drawn lines, "tendencies" are created.

The degree of light produces forms. Assja Turgenieff described how she, in relation to her own work, gradually started to understand what Steiner's comments meant. He said: "The strokes should never go with the form. They should have nothing to do with the form. In your case, the lines bend, if only slightly, along with the plastic shape. That is wrong. One should learn to shade independently of the form. So, never draw bent lines, otherwise lines are created after all. The line is a lie in the artistic process. The line can be used for the setup of a drawing, but no more than a builder uses scaffolding to construct a house. When the house is finished, the scaffolding is gone. So you should not start from a line. Eventually all traces of contours should disappear. The strokes should be very clearly visible, free, characteristic.

"But the strokes should have character and be as varied as possible; the point is to make them as different as possible—light, fixed, close together or wide apart, and so forth. That is what makes it artistic. If you want to obscure an area gradually, you can—as far as I am concerned—also cross through it, but very sharply, never under a straight corner. However, it is better to achieve obscuring by putting the strokes closer together or placing new strokes in between the others so that the direction of the lines remains the same. With this you liberate the drawn line, for the line is not beautiful anywhere in art."[24]

One can start with the simplest, for example, making a tree (and sunlight) appear on a lightly shaded background by gradually obscuring. Subjects such as botany or the Parsifal main lessons provide material for even more subjects. Working with this technique in eleventh grade is appropriate as an introduction at the beginning of the lessons where the young person discovers the inner development

24. See Assja Turgenieff: *The Imagery of the Goethanum Wimdows,* London: Rudolf Steiner Press, 1976.

and can deal with it. Shading is appropriate in secondary school, not in primary school!

Shading with color is painting (or embroidery) in effect and so cannot take the place of black and white shading. In this way shading in the above sense stands apart from other drawing techniques.

Sketching is practiced in all classes but particularly in eleventh grade. It is an aid to proper observation, enhancing perception. In the sketch and line drawing we emphasize what is formed, the lifeless reflection of life, an abstraction. In "dynamic drawing" however one tries to arrive at the form of, for example, an animal through the dynamics of hand and line through movement. Practice of dynamic line drawing is started alongside form-drawing in primary school.

In form-drawing we give the line its full value. Form-drawing as well as dynamic-drawing offers much developmental material for the secondary school pupil.[25] To the young person, approximately fourteen-years-old, it is important to discover how the form of the subject becomes visible with the light and how the line leads us away into abstraction, into the thinking world. Moving within the light is dealing with concrete reality in which the transcendental waits patiently to be revealed. We are moving in the field of the soul, where light and darkness constantly alternate, nothing is fixed. This is the field of shading and painting.

In the eleventh grade all aspects of drawing can be covered. For example, the pupils can work small scale in a self-bound sketchbook, at home and in the open. In class it is preferable to work large scale. Drawing plants, animals, people and each other can be alternated with assignments inspired more from the imagination. The shading

25. See Clausen and Riedel's *Zeichen, Sehen, Lernen.* While this book is not translated into English the illustrations are very clear and understandable.

technique lends itself well to this: wax crayons, charcoal, conté and pen can all be used.

* Basic exercise #14 for the teacher

Painting color circles is an instructive and inspiring exercise. The circle is painted without color boundaries or limits. In the color circle described here we allow the white and the black to meet each other fluidly on the sheet. From the movement they make, the colors appear.

From the top right we let the white condense via yellow into orange-vermilion-carmine, spiraling in areas towards the middle. At the bottom left stands the black. This black lights up the blue to the left and changes into purple on the right. On the left green is created in its meeting with yellow. In the center the blue stands sharply against the orange, the purple moves to the right. From its meeting with carmine, carnation/pink is created. The concentrated carnation (purple) connects with the concentrated vermilion, the most exciting spot in the painting. One could also start this exercise from the color red, with vermilion and carmine in the middle next to each other or in each other; one can also start from the black and the vermilion or from white and carmine.

The four image colors—white, green, black and carnation—stand around the lustre colors. Is everything balanced? This painting exercise can also be done using the wet-on-wet technique. This exercise is a basis, not only as preparation for twelfth grade, but also as a means to paint and observe the phenomena of color in general.

With this in mind we refer you again to Julius Hebing's color studies which are included in this book, providing a basic observation exercise for the inner preparation of the teacher. (see Chapter 6)

3.5 Painting in the twelfth grade

The summation

The sun shines on the year twelve pupil. Everything unites into a whole. Overviews of history, philosophy, religion, art history, chemistry, and so forth, help build an idea of humanity. The twelfth grade pupil, the young eighteen-year-old is not only seeking his/her freedom, but also self knowledge or the initial impulse towards it. "They experience creativity."

Usually six or more weeks of painting and an art history main lesson are the framework in which once again an overview of the development of art—with architecture used as a guiding principle—and aesthetics (Schiller, Beuys) is given. A painting curriculum, placing the human in a central position, can be given shape in many different ways. If we place the emphasis of "Gesamtkunst" [communal art], painting can then contribute to the creation of decors, book design, picture books for toddlers, posters, programs, and so forth. The teacher will use all kinds of approaches to show the pupils how artistic ideas can function and enrich. Alongside this we can place the human in a central position in portraits.

The human: studies of the head

Painting the human head is a special experience in twelfth grade. This activity has a considerable motivating effect for the entire class to paint together (just like we used in the old days in primary school). As a starting point we can take Steiner's sketch of a face and profile in blue and yellow. To this we add his remarks on the human carnation color and the physiognomy of the face reflecting the essence of the human being, so difficult to reproduce. We try to invite color and form to stand still for a little while.

We could also start from a wet-on-wet painting in a light blue environment in which spaces are left open for face and profile. The face can be colored in lightly with yellow. One can also work with a light blue ultramarine foundation and paint the surrounding area with Prussian blue, for example, and leave a space open for the face. Because this is not at all easy, we immediately do another one of these paintings with the same blue-yellow set up. We let both those colors melt together to green in the face, then place a layer of carmine from the neck over the cheek to the forehead. With this painting in mind, we remember the composition of the icon, the blushing red—a flower bud—life. We can pay attention to portraits through the centuries with the emphasis on the color carnation. Likewise we make a series of paintings in which the pink changes: more blue, more red, more yellow. This allows us to express age, temperament and tint. This should be experienced during the painting process. We start from a "pictorial" harmony of different colors as a background to the hair color and the dress color to express the moods.

It is best to work in pairs of wet-on-wet paintings, for example "toddler and old man" or "melancholy and cheerful" or "fair and brown." These paintings can be prepared in the previous lesson through blackboard sketches for physiognomy (sketchbook). When painting we leave open spaces for the positioning of the eyes, nose, mouth and ears until the color form indicates where they should be and then it becomes a matter of "drawing them in" with a light, mixed color. This is how we continue to yield to color and area. We also prevent ending up with a plastic shadow effect.

Not all work can be discussed, sometimes a pupil makes two paintings per lesson. From each completed assignment a few examples can be used in the next lesson to introduce an imminent new step and to motivate the pupils to improve self correction.

In the second half of the lessons we can start from several work methods. Preliminary exercises in the veiling technique are indispensable. Such preliminary exercises are concerned with the painting of pink as harmony of all colors and are (potentially) exercises in painting the pink between black and white. (see Chapter 6) Also in pure color mood faces are brought to the fore. It is a good opportunity to practice the most delicate veiling technique before starting on a face in a larger piece of work.

The further "independent" work on the theme "human or human countenance" is suitable for smaller groups. Sometimes we manage to fit this into the timetable. Using smaller groups enables us to pay attention to individual pupils when necessary. The pupils can work fairly independently on the same assignments, done wet-on-wet, but with variations and this time in the veiling technique. The setup is left to the pupil as are, of course, the color and form. The theme or the succession of themes is organized by the teacher. Wherever work can be done more individually, new assignments come up easily in dialogue between teacher and pupil. Sometimes it turns out that the pupil, especially in the beginning of twelfth grade, is not yet able to express his/her own ideas in a structured method or to sustain complete freedom of theme and choice of material in the available painting lessons, a freedom which can only be experienced by the young person after the twenty-first year. Exploring this field, however, should be possible in the twelfth grade. To this purpose different Waldorf teachers have developed varying didactic methods.

A sequel to this can be found in the "mother and child" subject. It can be developed in many ways. The teacher can point out the Madonna icons and, later, pictures of contemporary masters, and then, just as Steiner did in front of the class, show how this primordial image can be evoked from the harmony of blue, yellow and pink. The embracing gesture can be left to the pupils themselves, likewise the positioning of the eyes and the mouth with the pink-orange in the yellow and pink. "Painting out of the color" encourages pupils not to spend to much time on detail.

Many a twelfth grade pupil likes to occupy him/herself with this intimate image for some time. Personal preferences also vary. Painting a classmate or oneself, for example, can produce some precious results. Such a project demands preparation and build up, preparation in the sense of finding an inner attitude to start on such a grand project. The work done in previous years can be reviewed. Then portrait painting is done, from "experience" in the first instance the expressionist way, straight in wet-on-wet. A subsequent lesson is spent on observation. Not only sketches are done, but the colors of the complexion, the hair and the eyes, the position and the shape of the head, clothing, and the radiation effect are all observed and expressed or described by means of sketching or words. The painting itself, wet-on-wet or veiling, is not started until the next lesson. For a long time the painting is "color." The physiognomy is easier to work out if, at this late stage, a sketch is done on the basis of color composition, in which eyes, nose and mouth are given places. This should engender enough courage for the student to apply the characteristics that are within these colors. Jawlensky's work can help focus on "essence" and avoid exaggeration.

An attitude of personal dedication can be expected from the twelfth grade pupil. This is helped along, especially in the second half of the year, by the realization that they have nearly finished school working independently on the completion of their final projects.

There are different ways of allowing the seventeen- or eighteen-year-old to experience art in our time. In the art history lessons as well as in the painting lessons it is necessary to take big strides through the past to be able to understand the present. Experiencing the difference between Impressionism and Expressionism has its place in eleventh grade. In twelfth grade a short recap is possible of this in relation to what has been achieved in art history since then.

In particular the lives of individual artists and their personal oeuvre allow the student to take an interest in how art relates to the reality of life. Their own creations start to change after intense encounters with the spirit in the works of, for example, Warhol or Beuys.

This is how the pupils come through the general superficiality of their own experiences and develop an eye for the individual contribution made by each artist, each person, including the pupils themselves to the "Gesamtkunstwerk" culture. Biographies also have their place. Visits to museums, carefully guided and further discussed in class, can enrich these encounters. The teacher's task, especially in this lessons (often at the end of the year or in combination with a final school trip) is to not avoid a single personal conversation about art, art observation or experience of art, because many a young person forms ideas for future life. Is conversation not the smallest work of art?[26]

After all this, the pupil can speak from his/her own experience as a creative human about dedication and superficiality, about honesty and dishonesty in the creative attitude, about human and divine creation, about the connection between science, art and religion. The teacher, renewing the pedagogy in practice every time from that same creative attitude, can contribute to the development of the freely creative person.

---

26. See *Goethe's Standard of the Soul* (includes an English text of *The Green Snake and the Beautiful Lily*), New York: Anthroposophic Press, 1979.

4. Additional Aspects
for the Didactics of the Painting Lesson

4.1 Lesson preparation, post-discussion, temperaments
Directions for elementary school

The preparation of the painting lesson contains several essential elements. A statement by Steiner immediately points to one of the most important ones: One should be able to think equally well in colors and forms as one can in concepts, in thoughts,[27] a task which naturally goes beyond just one painting lesson. Years of working with color in all its facets is the basis for the necessary skill of "thinking in color." Study and self motivation, observation and the practice of teaching build up responsible and conscious use of the painting assignments. Each small step inspires the next step. Specifically the connection between insight and practice necessary in this field of expertise encourages further study. The teacher starting in first grade provides the opportunity to travel together with the children on the path of color as an expression of soul mood up to the colors we can observe outside in nature.

By painting the assignment prior to the lesson, the teacher gains experience and increases his/her skill to explain the setup and the directions to the children. Sometimes several exercises are

---

27. See Steiner's *Architektur, Plastik und Malerei des Ersten Goetheanum*, January 25, 1920.

needed to obtain the proper result. The assignment always aligns with previous and future exercises and fits in with the children's experience and potential. Once the assignment is clear to the teacher, he/she can ask the questions whether it is suitable, whether this assignment should be painted or drawn. Once again we point out the considerable distinction between color area and line. On the one hand the feeling world is addressed via the color area. On the other hand the line appeals to the consciousness, the two-dimensional next to the one-dimensional. (see Chapter 5.1)

After preparing the paint (basic exercise 1 for the teacher) the actual lesson can start. In primary school pairs of children share paint and water jar. Each pupil has his/her own painting board, paper, sponge, brush and possibly a painting overall or apron.

Preparing and passing out the equipment/materials can be done in several ways. In the break the children can take turns getting everything ready. This can also be organized for the whole class. The equipment can be shared out row by row. Clearing away can be done in the same way. Order and quiet are important, as well as good organization. After a number of lessons the children will know exactly what is expected of them. Putting the painting boards with wet paintings into a painting-cupboard, in which all boards can be horizontally stored, is a most convenient way of allowing the paintings to dry slowly. Drying them on the floor in the front or back of the classroom or on tables, if there is not another lesson, is also possible. Each class will find its own practical way of working.

The long path of preparation for the teacher is gradually reduced as more experience is gained. The set time in the week also provides the teacher with some grip. Rhythm is healthy for both pupil and teacher. Choosing a day for painting, preferably not the last day of the week, has the advantage of putting the teacher in a better position to observe the aftereffects. Using the night and sleep in relation to the effect of color on the child is important. Working in the two-dimensional sphere has its specific effect on the etheric-astral territory. In his first lecture on "General human biology as a basis for pedagogy," Steiner discusses the importance of healthy sleep and breathing in connection with learning. This is one of the reasons why it is important that the class teacher give the painting classes, throughout the years, instead of "someone from the outside."

This is equally important in connection with the post-discussion of the painting work. During the painting lesson the children's soul windows open up. The soul still expresses itself directly and purely in the painting. Every child does this, even when overshadowed by circumstances. Each child "shows his/her colors." How can we best make observations applicable with regards to pedagogy? How does the child paint, how does he pick up the assignment, how does he get started, how does he deal with the equipment, how does he hold the pencil, which movements stand out, which colors and forms are emphasized? Does the child crawl onto the paper with his tongue sticking out or is he sitting back, working lightly in a detached way? Is the brush pushed through the paper or does it slide inaudibly across the surface of the paper? Is the work dry or wet? Is it a strain for the child? Sweaty hands? A considerable range of observational opportunities arise which the teacher can write down at home prior to the lesson. After the lesson he/she tries to recall a number of pupils and makes pertinent notes. Undoubtedly there are still many gaps here.

Practice soon pays off however. These observations are incredibly important for working with the four temperaments. Each child is inclined towards a certain temperament. Is the child choleric, melancholic, sanguine or phlegmatic? Does he have different temperaments or a mixture of these? Observations through the seasons and throughout the lessons give indications, with which the teacher can get started.

Let us first view the class work as a whole. The teacher has to create order in the colorful "chaos." The work of the pupils can in fact, be divided into four large groups (we're not referring to the temperaments here). Imagine we manage to group the work in this way: four piles of work. When hanging up the work we can still place many "dubious cases" in between the various extremes. For example, we could start with hanging the light paintings at the top right, while the ones with more powerful colors hang diagonally down at bottom left. Then the paintings with vague forms (the more fluid ones without boundaries) will have a space more to the right of the wall and the strongly formed more to the left. This is how work out an initial order and the eye can slide from right to left and bottom to top and meet the transitions in color. This continuum is pleasant to the eye and evokes a feeling of pleasure (sense of life) especially for the children. In a class of thirty pupils all aspects will be amply represented. Or does the class as a whole tend towards a certain direction? Often a certain balance is present, which would not be the case if we looked at a random collection of paintings.

By sticking to a certain order when hanging up the paintings the individual child's achievement is seen as part of a whole. Discussion needs to start the next day or a little later in the week. To start off with we can review what the actual assignment was as a foundation for the painting lesson and choose which painting best represents this. A moment of viewing and whispering has arrived. Give the children time to orient themselves! "Where does blue look forward to the arrival of yellow?" "Where has red put a spell on yellow?" "Can anyone see orange sitting in a corner?" are examples for the lower classes. From these questions and the ensuing conversation both teacher and pupils develop a new color language, a new vocabulary as they learn to describe without judging. Contributions by the children are important. During the class conversation the teacher encourages the children. "What do you feel?" or "Did you choose that one too?" After all, colors are beings manifesting themselves in the most divergent ways: in strength of color and dynamics, in their mutual composition, in color tone, in light and darkness, and so forth. In the lower classes a color sign language arises. In the higher classes we can refer to natural phenomena. "Can we talk of a night mood in the pine forest?" The class conversation is also appropriate for other subjects. A listening attitude should be built up, hence the need for a degree of discipline in conversation. The teacher holds back and guides where necessary. He/she tries to lead the class back to the phenomenon itself, because even a conversation about red and yellow can soon turn into a chat about the neighbor's dog.

Finally, let us return to the temperaments. For a more elaborate description we refer you to the many lectures about the subject by Steiner.[28] Basically in the four temperaments we distinguish four fundamental moods in the soul, created (like the green from yellow and blue), from different currents. The way in which these currents interweave is a determining factor in the temperament color of the child. It is up to the educator to observe and recognize them and by means of education achieve a long term balance. In her book *Formenzeichnen*[29] Hildegard Bethold-Andrae connects the temperaments to form-drawing. Beyond her work we can see the

---

28. See Steiner's booklet *Four Temperaments*, New York: Anthroposophic Press, 1987, and Magda Lissau's *The Temperaments and the Arts*, Fair Oaks, CA: AWSNA Publications, 2003.
29. See Ernst Kranisch, Margrit Jünemann, and Hildegard Bethold-Andrae's book *Formenzeichen (Form Drawing)*, not yet translated into English.

four paintings of the four different temperaments printed in the book *Waldorf Education* by Frans Carlgren.

In many ways understanding the temperament is the real key to the recognition and treatment of extreme one-sidedness in a child. The temperament is expressed in the paintings via the choice and composition of colors, in the extension of the color areas and in the child's approach to the work. There is no ready-made recipe. We can, however, give guidelines that can help the teacher search and research.

The *choleric* child is inclined to use strong colors, the areas are formed, but are not always contrastingly opposed. Inner dynamics stand out. The *phlegmatic* person is the master of color transitions. Use of color can be strong here too. The unity of the painting stands out. The *melancholic* child usually wants to handle the colors very carefully. His work is usually a little dry and strongly bordered. It does not flow. Stronger colors are sometimes present like lead on the paper. Mobility in color form and gesture characterize the work of the *sanguine* child. Surprising color nuances can result. He tends towards the too wet, the unformed. No one child has one temperament exclusively, but often one dominates. A good pedagogue however does not label a child. He/she weighs and balances, observes again and has discussions with him/herself and the other colleagues. There are moments in all education when expressions of temperament come to the fore. The painting lesson is one such moment, because there the children reveal themselves naturally in color and form.

The teacher leads and relaxes at the same time. Experience shows this paradox can be bridged. When talking about painting Rudolf Steiner did not have childlike art in mind. We are always concerned with elements, directly inspired and connected with "Grand Art." A weekly drop in the colorful "bowl of the soul" of the child contributes to a healthy upbringing.

High school level

Most of Steiner's recommendation for high school have already been mentioned in the chapters describing the curriculum for the respective classes. His school sketches give examples of which themes and how these should be worked out, starting from the color. His remarks about the riches that Dürer's etchings offer in the way of development material for the older pupil have also been mentioned before. "Always start from the simplest [idea]" is one of his mottoes, which has kept its meaning through all these years, but which does not mean "always the same from the beginning." It is important for the secondary school teacher to continue to mold the elementary aspects Steiner mentions into new work forms and themes adjusted to pupil and class, to pursue topical interests and to build on to the rich technical experience which the pupils bring with them from primary school.

The teacher will use class and individual discussions to assist pupils with the assignment. Avoid judging and denouncing. By means of asking questions the teacher makes sure that the pupil learns to observe, contemplate and judge, and is able to effect change.

In high school the work of the pupils should be based around a common theme. The fourteen- to eighteen-year-old, however, is strongly focused on personal achievement, so more variety can be brought into the work via discussion.

The teacher keeps the discussions from becoming long deep digging sessions, yet allows for sincere honest expression. In each lesson at any time and in any manner, moments of contemplation can be scheduled in, which have a stimulating effect. For example, one project is discussed, or two projects are compared to clarify a point. The work of all pupils can also be hung up or laid out on the floor. The pupils can observe silently or, on the basis of a directed question, observe and consider together.

It has great value for the pupil to notice that the teacher is familiar with his/her work and development. This is why the pupils' folders should be regularly perused. (One does not always know beforehand when a certain helpful hint can be given to the pupil; sometimes it is better to keep quiet.) The developing individual is still vulnerable in his/her newly released astrality.

In elementary school the temperaments become visible in painting. In secondary school further identification and study need to be developed from a pedagogical perspective.

We have mentioned before Steiner's recommendations to make the assignments in pairs (of paintings) or next to each other, for example, "sunrise" and "sunset." This way of working evokes an investigative, studious attitude. Art and science complement each other in such matters. Art can instruct us in the field of form and design. In the art lesson we are not just dealing with the talented artist, but also with potential scientists and craftsmen. All dispositions can be catered to in the practical art subjects by working specifically on these two aspects of each assignment: research and design (for example, making picture books or posters). In the case of the visual arts this includes the finishing (frame) and the location within a space/room (which painting fits where?)

4.2 Curative and pedagogical painting

The classroom door opens. The art therapist beckons to a child. The other pupils carry on with their work. This child is given full attention for a while. She paints. What she paints can vary considerably. How she paints matters a great deal: delicate or strong colors, wet/dry, vice versa, small or large format. How does the child work the brush and so forth. The therapist's choice of words and his/her relationship with colors and material is balanced, respectful, loving. The child has the opportunity to express him/herself during painting. The therapist is there to guide each step. He/she observes intensely and controls the process.

In art therapy a choice is made between clay-modeling, form-drawing, painting, or an area that lies in between in consultation with a doctor. Each artistic activity has a certain effect in the soul area and from the soul the essence of humanity is nourished and healed. Working with color and water generally has a liberating, loosening effect. How we fall asleep and wake up is influenced by the images which are processed via our thoughts into the soul. Painting means enriching the world of images. Dealing with color strengthens the quality of feeling or the sensitivity. Atmosphere, mood, gesture and/or tone are beginning to be part of reality. If a rigidity appears in the feeling life, then painting, for example, makes the child more receptive.

Art therapy must support medical treatment. Consultation with a doctor is therefore imperative. Diagnosis, as well as pre- and post-therapy discussions usually include the class teacher.

Painting, as described in this book (specified per class), also holds a certain therapeutic value for each child in the class. In the pedagogy arising from the anthroposophical spiritual science each subject has its therapeutic effect. However therapy in the sense of art therapy is out of the question when it comes to the class. By emphasizing the therapeutic aspect too strongly one could use painting as a healing "bath" or "medicine," and that is not its primary function.

In current Waldorf practice it is right and necessary to encourage painting, but not for its therapeutic value. Painting as a subject within the curriculum serves a pedagogical purpose. Together with the other subjects it combines to form the complete person. In school and in class we are concerned with processing the subject matter in a healthy manner; the healthy incarnation of the young person is our aim.

One could find that certain methods in art therapy are a help to a certain class; for example, treating the equipment/material with care, painting certain shapes in a certain color mood or technique, even painting images (one paints the sun, the grass etc.) as in curative pedagogy. Yet what is "appropriate" in therapy is not automatically appropriate in class. The child–therapist, therapist–child relationship is the healing base from which all sorts of treatments become "therapy." The teacher aims for a different, pedagogical objective. He/she makes choices as to the content and the method with the child's phase of development in mind. He/she builds up, links up with what has gone before, and prepares the new material. In short, he/she carefully processes within the framework of the "grand curriculum." Class or group one-sidedness, individual differences between the children, are carried along with the current of assignments and variations in method which painting offers. It provides material which stirs the healthy child.

Cooperation between therapist and teacher is of mutual benefit and will help in finding suitable methods for "healing" a child.

Once again we refer you to the example of the two active color-form-exercises, as described by Steiner in Oxford, in connection with [elements] of one-sidedness/ "holding everything in the head" and the "not sinking in of the subject matter."[30]

------

30. See Steiner's *The Spiritual Ground of Education*, New York: Steiner Books, 2003. See also the sections on curriculum for the third grade. A chronological overview of Rudolf Steiner's quotes as regards therapy and painting can be found in the book *Farbenerkenntniss*, GA, 291A, pages 452–456, not yet translated into English.

5. Use of Color
in Other Lessons and in the School Building

5.1 Drawing, form-drawing, crafts, needlework and drama

In painting, color is the means for education, but for aesthetic, functional, and pedagogical reasons it plays an important role in all aspects of education.

In free drawing, it has been pointed out, color is left open/free as much as possible. The teacher can encourage the use of color but leaves the choice up to the child. Generally speaking the pupil will choose coloring in a line drawing. Black is sometimes necessary when there is coal or a black car in the drawing. This color should then be available. One should however protect the child to a certain extent from the black, because it suggests the absence of light and is not a color in that sense.

From third grade onward the child can be helped to color drawings "richly," because at this age they tend not to. We do this by making a drawing together now and again, which we build up into areas, but more strongly formed than in painting. This we call drawing in the manner of a painting style. It is especially important for board drawings (in the lower classes) to be established this way—with lots of area and color and with as few lines and contours as possible.

In form-drawing the line, the fixed movement is the means of expression. Color in this case is of secondary importance. In certain assignments (e.g., the temperaments) color can support the form. In other words, in form-drawing we do not use color to just "brighten it up."

Taught in all classes, needlework is a subject, in which the "sense of color" is particularly awakened. Whatever is produced in the needlework lesson ends up, no matter how simple, as a useful product. This makes needlework one of the subjects in which, from a young age, the function becomes visible through the color in the form of the object, for example, motifs on caps/hats and bags, or the matching of inside and outside in, for example, a slipper. In bookbinding matching of cover and content is also emphasized.

A remarkable way of working with light and color is the making of transparencies. One can bring the color mood into the class by covering a window in certain colors of silk paper. In this way a festival or a different theme can be depicted. For the pupils this is a colorful activity, standing in front of the window or working on a glass plate with light underneath it. It is important to prevent the creation of a gaudy piece of work. This is done by using overlapping layers and by keeping an eye on light and dark spots. When applying this technique to lanterns and decors for phantasmagorias, the same insight from the teacher in the identity of color is required as that which we have discussed in painting. How do the colors fit in with, for example, the mood of a scene in a play?

Identifying with color in the costumes, the props and the decors helps us tune into the actual drama. Color has a very strong effect here and it is important that each teacher has at least an elementary awareness of this.

For preschool children and lower class pupils we make rewarding use of beeswax. The children love to give shape to their rich imagination with this material. Choice of color consequently requires the greatest possible freedom. Badly separated, mixed or grey colors are much less popular than those with obvious character. So we keep these colors separate to enjoy for awhile. In the higher classes transparencies can be made with colored kneading wax on glass plates. In order to make something visibly clear, we generally use a great deal of color. Choice of color can be significant in its own right. At school we continue to try using colors in a useful way, e.g., on the blackboard and in the main lesson books. Excess of color restricts the function. Dearth of color stresses intellectualism, negates interest and enthusiasm, and switches off feeling. Color, form and function in balance produce beauty in all daily things. In designing self-made lesson reports, in main lesson books, and in all other written work the pupil is encouraged to create beauty. The teacher gives the example and advises; the pupil acts and learns.

5.2 Rudolf Steiner's color advice for the school building

In Waldorf schools the attempt is made to guide and support the development of the pupils by making certain color choices for the classrooms, corridors and other spaces. Artistic and pedagogical viewpoints play a large part in this. The aesthetic education comprises three large working areas; the pupils move around in an artistically formed environment. Pedagogy in its entirety is practiced artistically and the latter comprises the consciously guided development in creation and enjoyment. In this way aesthetics mediate between the spiritual and the material; art constitutes a link between processes in the spiritual realm and the physical-material realm. In Schiller's *Letters on the Aesthetic Education of Mankind*, such thoughts are expressed and developed.[31] He saw art as a subject in which the

31. Schiller, Friedrich. *Letters on the Aesthetic Education of Mankind*, New York: Frederick Unger Publishing, 1963.

human both creates and experiences the joy of the creation—here we discover the spiritual connection between matter and form. It is definitely not immaterial how the creation is formed and in particular which colors are used.

Color constitutes an essential part of the environment, together with the architecture of the school building itself, color in service of the education of the young person. In Chapter 1 of this book we covered many aspects of color. How can we deal with these ideas in such a way that they will not degenerate into fixed principles, but can be constantly tested in practice? How do we employ this knowledge to surround the pupil with a colorful and appropriate mood? After all, they spend a great deal of time inside the school building.

When designing the interior of the first Waldorf school, Steiner gave a series of directions for the color of the classroom walls. He was aiming for transparent colors, colors with a lively character that would allow a wall to "breathe."[32] An artistically-developed colored environment has a harmonizing and even healing effect. Suitable materials were not easily available at the time. These were developed during the construction of the first Goetheanum. Steiner said: "We should succeed again in not just watching the colors and applying them here and there as an external feature, but we must live with the colors, be part of the inner life force of color. We cannot reach this aim by just studying while painting, how one or another color acts. We can only do this by submerging our souls in the direct flow, experiencing them vividly in our minds."

A wall painted in transparent colors does not seem to have such strong boundaries as a wall painted with a solid color. When "veiling"

---

32. See Steiner's *Colour*, London: Rudolf Steiner Press, GA 291, twelve lectures, 2001.

the walls, the space has an atmospheric effect. It widens, becomes more spacious; this is different for each color. Spaces painted in this new way do not have a direct effect on people's imaginative powers, but leave them free. With this veiling technique many nuances can be made in color strength and color transition. Steiner advised painting the classroom in one color, warm and therefore enveloping colors for the younger children and cooler colors for the secondary school classes. He developed four different color schemes for three different locations in Europe, taking into consideration climate, landscape and natural character of the pupils in southern and northern Germany and in England. In order to activate the feeling world of northern German pupils, Steiner chose warm red-orange colors in the first six years of school after Kindergarten. But we notice that with the colors given for a London school, no choice was made for yellow in between the orange and green. The naturally more sensitive, lively North American child rather needs bluish tints around him/her to be able to concentrate better and in doing so promote the thinking process.

The situation in the Netherlands is somewhere in between these two recommendations. The schemes are included at the end of this chapter. The wood barracks in Stuttgart, where the first school started, had one color throughout the first eight classes: bluish lilac. Wherever possible the school furniture was painted and stained the same color. The curtains were given a lighter tint than the walls. All this created a whole color impression for the pupils. These directions are used in Waldorf schools all over the world. Each country develops its own color use, material and technique, fitting in with the nature of the people. Dealing with this information artistically means that everyone needs to observe and to ask: "How does the color affect the children?" Applying it without understanding why or incongruent with the underlying reasons contradicts the method Steiner advocates.

With the "lazure" or veiling technique we are talking about a watercolor technique usually on a white foundation. The original color of the foundation is covered, but the structure can remain visible. To obtain stronger colors we can take a light tinted foundation as a basis, because it is technically difficult to apply the veils equally up to great color strength. Each new veil should be a thin, weak layer of paint coloring the wall a little with each application. The working of the color is thereby intensified and differentiated.

When one particular color is used exclusively, the wall can have too much strength and effect. It is a painter's secret to give the wall some thin layers of a complementary color in the later stages. This reduces the shining character of the color, so that it does not force itself on the observer. A yellow wall, for example, can be given some lilac or purple veils. This makes for a very special color effect. Everyone should try this out and experience it for themselves. Only from observation can these contrasting colors be chosen; they have to be applied with much care and attention to achieve the desired result.

The importance of a good choice of colors for a certain age group to support their development is clearly signaled by Ernst Weissert in *Erziehungskunst* of June 1952: "The question about the children's environment, how the spaces in which they spend their school hours are formed, is even more important today than before. Nowadays a number of visual impressions force themselves onto the young child. A speedy development of observation is encouraged. Questions which occupied Steiner from the pedagogical and medical points of view are turned into actual assignments: to address the child's needs by having a suitable design of class space and by painting transparent colors, which have a calming or an activating effect on the child."

The four color schemes as advised by Rudolf Steiner are composed as follows:

Goetheschool in Hamburg (1925):

grades 1, 2 and 3	red, gradually reduced in strength each class
grades 4, 5 and 6	orange, gradually reduced in strength each class
seventh grade	yellow
eighth grade	green
ninth grade	lighter green
tenth grade	blue
eleventh grade	blue tending towards violet
twelfth grade	violet
eurythmy hall	violet
physics classroom	green
music classroom	lilac

The Stuttgart barracks, the second color for the new building in Stuttgart (1923):

first grade	bluish lilac, red
second grade	bluish lilac, orange
third grade	bluish lilac, yellow
fourth grade	bluish lilac, light green
fifth grade	bluish lilac, green tending towards blue
sixth grade	bluish lilac, blue
seventh grade	bluish lilac, indigo
eighth grade	bluish lilac, violet
ninth grade	bluish lilac, violet
tenth grade	bluish lilac, lilac

eleventh grade	bluish lilac, lilac
eurythmy hall	bluish lilac, mallow
physics classroom	bluish lilac, blue
corridors	bluish lilac, lilac
music classroom	indigo, red-like lilac
gym hall	bluish lilac, red-like lilac
doctor's room	bluish lilac, red-like
handicraft	bluish lilac, orange
needlecraft	bluish lilac, light violet towards red

London (1925):

kindergarten	red-yellow
first grade	orange
second grade	green
third grade	darker green
fourth grade	blue green
fifth grade	light blue
sixth grade	darker blue
eurythmy hall	light violet
corridors	yellow

6. Sources

Only where perceptive knowing steps
One will find the gate
Which, for the world of the soul
Opens up real life
The soul can forge the key
When she grows strong within herself,
Through the battle waged by world powers
On her own territory
With human powers;
When she drives out her own strength
The sleep which shrouds
The power of knowledge to the
Limit of her senses in darkness of spirit.
                    – Rudolf Steiner
                    Whitsun motto

6.1 Rudolf Steiner's color lectures

Goethe's theory of color as a basis for teacher and pupil

The term "theory of color" suggests a degree of restriction by ideas alone. Newton's color theories (and its many variations) and Goethe's are the best known. Goethe's theory was written as a response to Newton's. While Newton divides light, creating colors, Goethe demonstrates that colors come to the fore through an interaction of light and darkness. Newton's point of view may have had considerable success (e.g., in science and technology), but through a close study of colors, Goethe's approach, in particular his empirical methods, takes up an important position in pedagogy and art.

Now that Goethe's theory of color has been translated into English, the words and method of research of the scientist/scholar-poet-statesman are available to the teacher with a special interest in color.

A step by step procession through the theory of color, as structured by Goethe, is the basis for his conclusive thoughts about the sense-moral effect of color set forth in the last chapter. Steiner puts this all together in his lectures on color.

In the chapter on "Physiological Colors" Goethe covers after-images and colored shadows. These are the phenomena most linked to the eye. In the subsequent chapters colors are not directly linked to us. Goethe calls these the *physical* colors. Here we are concerned with the atmospheric colors (the blue sky, the evening red, and so forth) and the prismatic colors. When covering the chemical colors (acids and bases), Goethe stresses the systematic diffusion in a red and a blue spectrum, and in the next chapter he joins the colors together to the six-part color circle.

The primordial phenomenon of division into polarities and the aiming for unity in a third, higher element, is described by Goethe as fruitful and related to other disciplines, such as philosophy, physics, painting and others.

Subsequently, after characterizing the colors separately, he gives names to the color combinations which influence each other: the *harmonic*—opposite each other in the color circle; the *characteristic* color combinations—consisting of colors which join in a triangle within the six-part color circle (yellow, blue, red and purple, orange, green). The *characterless* combinations are next to each other in the circle, like yellow and green. Steiner's recommendations for the first painting lesson "yellow and blue beside yellow and green" and relevant guidelines are based on these "types." Finally, after his directions for the painter, Goethe provides some examples which explain the symbolic value of colors. Purple for example is majesty. He points out the primordial phenomenon of color and the inherent spiritual aspect.

Each Waldorf pupil is introduced, around the twelfth year, to the phenomena of light and darkness. This introduction takes place in the physics main lessons. To give an impression of what the pupils learn in this lessons, here is an overview.

- The phenomena that occur when we look at white on black or black on white. A black dot of equal size on a white area seems smaller than the same dot in white on a black area. Light comes towards us and black gives way.
- The physical colors. Creating the morning- and evening red and the sky-blue by obscuring the light and lighting up the darkness.
- The after images, referred to as "colorful images" by Goethe. When we observe a color, we observe the contrasting color (on our retina) either on the surrounding color or on a different area, to which we subsequently direct our glance.
- The prismatic colors. We perceive these when looking through cut glass or another light refracting medium (e.g. water-prism) at a light-dark boundary.
- The colored shadows. Goethe covers these together with the phenomenon of after images. The experiments, which make the colored shadows visible continue to astound the observer.

The setup of the above mentioned experiments can be found in Julius Hebing's *Mensch, Welt und Farbe* in the chapter on "Physiological Colors," at present not translated into English.

In sixth grade this introduction should emphasizes the "wonder" of color through observation. In twelfth grade, when the theory of color is once again covered as part of the theory of light in the physics lessons, wonder is not enough. The teacher will make the pupils aware of the rules by means of observation, so that they leave school with an idea of the laws and wisdom contained within color and light. So from sixth grade onwards one can revisit this experience when painting and drawing in black and white. In twelfth grade it is interesting to establish the connection between painting and physics and/or to make important phenomena visible to the painter in actual painting.

Rudolf Steiner's color lectures. The lustre colors

In developing the theory of color both Goethe and Steiner had the needs of the painter-artist as a first consideration. Goethe established in the last chapter of his *Theory of Color*, the connection between colors and spiritual beings. He makes sure he is not considered "vague" and leaves it at that.

Steiner goes further and describes how the human can connect intensely with color, how through intensive observation and absorption of color, she/he can meet the spiritual being working within it and that in so doing "will make important discoveries in the future." Steiner mentions experiences in the intense observation of red, orange, yellow, green and blue. With red he gives the description of "form created from color." Here the transition from vermilion red to a carmine red expands into a star shape. The vermilion we experience as an effect of "the wrath of God" and the carmine "makes one learn to pray." "There is mercy!" This is how Steiner describes the inner experiences in connection with external observation. For the artist, he says, these experiences provide the foundation on which he/she can work creatively "from the color" in the future.

Goethe described the use of color perspective, that is using blue to evoke a "going away" and red/yellow a "coming towards us," from his own experiences. Steiner explains how humanity since the Renaissance left behind the use of color perspective and how, in our time, we are able to return to it. He also points out the pedagogical value of living in color perspective and through this *geschmeidig werden* (becoming receptive) to the child's soul.[33]

As does Goethe, Steiner once more stresses how with yellow and blue the space-filling, radiating element of the yellow places itself opposite the enclosing, space-creating blue. The red stands between these two as the active color resting within itself. Steiner termed these *Glanzfarben* (lustre colors), because of their active character. This is how he relates them to the human.

- yellow is the lustre of the spirit or of the spiritual, of the I" element;
- blue is the lustre of the soul;
- red is the lustre of the living.

Goethe connects the three main colors by creating from them a six-part color circle. One can imagine blue and yellow flowing together into green and on the other side red and blue united intensely in purple. The colors are independent beings, but through

---

33. See Steiner's *The Child's Changing Consciousness*, New York: Anthroposophical Press, GA 306, 1996. See also: *Farben Erkenntnis* GA 291A, not yet translated into English.

them a constant movement also becomes noticeable, as one color blends into another.

In painting, we are continually dealing with "being" (limited) and "becoming" (unlimited) through the effect of color. Colors meet and either intensify or evaporate, a different color emerges, a new mood is created. One could say, where there is a boundary, the influence of astrality is more obvious. It is the realm in which one thing differentiates itself from the other. A continuous movement-without-obstructions in colors is the more etheric side of the process. Thus the unconscious flowing movement complements the consciousness-creating, limiting aspect in each color experience.

The image colors

An entirely new aspect in Steiner's lectures is his description of the image colors. The term "image color" stands for reflected or shadow color. We are talking about white, black, green and peach blossom. These are the colors which distinguish themselves from the lustre colors red, blue and yellow. In the case of green and peach blossom they form the connection between the two separate sections of the spectrum: the red-yellow and the blue.

"Image color directions" become particularly meaningful in the painting of minerals, plants, animals and people. The image color, the image quality of color, is most clearly observed in the plant green. The origin of the plant essence from the earth's moon development period, the moon-phase, is expressed in the green. In the way moonlight is an image, a reflection of sunlight, so to green depicts life, but is lifeless, the lifeless image of life.

When Steiner describes the image color as images for the essential part of the human being (life, death, soul, and spirit, for example), their mutual alliance becomes even clearer. He refers to the green as "the lifeless image of life" (e.g., the color of plants), the peach blossom color "the living image of the soul" (e.g., the skin of a healthy baby), white or light "the soul image of the spirit (e.g., a white cloth, the indication of a purified soul), black "the spiritual image of the lifeless" (e.g., a black garment to express the impersonal, the unassailable). From black via green and rose to white, a color movement runs through the realms of nature, from the lifeless (mineral) to the living (plant) to the soul (animal) and the spirit (human). Each image color is thus described as a reflection of something just as each shadow needs an illuminant and a shadow caster, the image colors can be understood. With black "lifeless" is the source, and the spirit is the object casting the shadow. "Object" in this sense is too physical. We should, as it were, see "lifeless" expressed in the spiritual. That produces black. In other words:

- the shadow of the lifeless in the spirit is black;
- the shadow of life in the lifeless is green;
- the shadow of the soul in the living is peach blossom;
- the shadow of the spirit in the soul is white.

Image colors therefore, according to Steiner, represent reflection and are a contrast to the rational explanation of color essences.

Painting the realms of minerals, plants, animals, and the human

When we want to paint the plant green, we can emphasize the image character of the green by painting it darker than it is in reality and on top of this applying a yellow-white layer (lustre of the spirit), enveloping the plant being as if filled with light. In class, these directions are easily followed. Initially it is better to spend time on the green, intensifying the shadow character by going over with white-yellow to provide unity in the whole picture. Two paintings, one with and one without a yellow top layer, seen next to each other clearly show this. This description of the realm of plants includes flowers and fruits. These can also be painted darker, with image character, and finally finished with a veil of yellow-white.

Colored crystals are the most outspoken form of mineral. If the plant were illumined from the outside, the lustre of the mineral comes to meet us from the inside. No matter which color we speak of, the light or lustre character has to be evoked in the painting, otherwise the object will not have mineral character. In the third color lecture Steiner continues and recommends that the surface should be thoroughly brought to lustre through white light to let the essence appear, to make the mineral shine. All color in the realm of minerals, image colors included, should have lustre character. That is why with minerals we should let the white of the paper shine through everything.

All animals typically have a quick-tempered inner world. This animation is expressed by the blue as "lustre of the soul." In practice this means that we initially paint the animal a little lighter or more yellow-red than in reality and that we cover this color with a blue veil. This, in combination with the plant world forming the animal's environment, requires a finishing touch of yellow-white over the plant green which changes into a blue layer of the animal. In the case of an animal representation of color we consequently speak of image lustre, a lustre which has become image. With the plant the image color is brought to lustre: lustre image, an image leading to lustre.

The human is the image of his/her own essence. The essence of the human is image. The spiritual pervades the human essence. This is expressed in carnation or pink or peach blossom. Everything that is color as regards the human, including clothing, has image character. In this case we do not paint white transparent lustre, but we subdue the color, let each color become image. For example, when it concerns people we take away the radiant force of yellow by painting over it with the complementary color. The incarnate (the color of the face) is created from a lively meeting between light and darkness, with a soft red shining through. This meeting can be translated into yellow and blue and therefore green. Green is the result of that meeting between light and dark. From yellow, blue and red the image color carnation (incarnate) is created. Through the centuries many artists have sought the recipe for the lively color of the human skin. Steiner approaches it in a completely new way: "In the lively weaving of light in darkness, white in black, a soft purple red radiates: living incarnate."

So in Steiner's lectures on color are a direct continuation of the work of Goethe, with a subsequent completely new approach to color experience, appealing to new skills, which can be developed by the contemporary human.

Developing and continuing color research. The work of Julius Hebing

Painters and scientists, but also teachers, control the continuation of color research. Nowadays this is a vast area of technology. The study of effects of color on people in color psychology, therapy, and advertising is mixed with developments in the field of the arts, where color and ideas about color influence such things as architecture, stage lighting, fashion and design. Ongoing debate continues between the more materialistic adherents and those following a spiritual science approach. The works of the "Farbenlabor" in Dornach and the "Vereniging voor Kleurenstudie" in the Netherlands stand out.

For lesson preparation and a Goethe-like continuation of the study of colors, the work of Julius Hebing is a true treasure chest.

His series of magazines *Welt, Farbe und Mensch* is the result of a conscientious research by the painter arising from Steiner's color lectures. Entirely in line with Goethe's scientific attitude, Hebing has converted many phenomena into visible color examples. His work at the Stuttgart Lehrenseminar [teacher training] has profoundly influenced teachers at Waldorf schools around the world. The publishing of *Welt, Farbe und Mensch* and Hebing's diaries *Lebenskreise, Farbenkreise* are indispensable to any school library (unfortunately, these have not yet been translated into English). The first one is an extensive study reworked by Hildegard Berthold-Andrae. It is a clear manual exploring through experimentation the various areas of continued color research. The folder of color prints is itself an impressive testimony to the work of the artist who dedicated his whole life to the study of colors. Steiner's statements in the first edition of Goethe's *Theory of Color* in 1891 are an encouragement to carry on research into color.

In the circle around and following Hebing, artists, scientists, teachers, therapists, psychologists, philosophers, and others occupy themselves with this work. The color lectures form a base on which the further discovery of colors can be carried on in the future. In this way, lustre and image colors form one vivid interplay between colors in Steiner's vision. Julius Hebing has worked on the lustre colors and the vivid linking up with the image colors. It is an image worth frequent study and interpretation.

In his study Hebing further considers Steiner's remark that experience of color has developed through the centuries and is still developing. It is known that the Greeks were not (yet) able to discern blue. This is evident from their use of words. Steiner states that the Greeks did not discern the blue element because they were still more involved in the red element. In our time, we are indeed able to experience blue. The conscious seeing and/or naming of colors, which we can distinguish nowadays and which we use in our daily language, is not a matter of course for each nation. Thus Hebing describes that, at the time of rising colonialism, people were discovered in Africa who had hardly any words in their vocabulary for blue and green . The words they used corresponded more with black and grey. For the warmer colors however, they often had a plethora of words. The shepherd nation, like the Ovahereros, had a considerable preference for and interest in the colors of their herds. They were able to distinguish between green and blue, but they found no need to express this in language. They knew twenty-six different expressions for the colors and markings of their herds. Europeans researching the color vocabulary kept running into this phenomenon. The "primitives" had no essential interest in the colors in free nature (e.g. the blue sky or the green trees). Green, blue and violet were interchanged with colors like black and grey. A tribe was discovered who had only one word for green and blue: *enoli*, meaning fresh or raw, similar to the way we might say, "He is still green, he's not ready for it yet." When this tribe learned about the preparation of the color indigo as a blue coloring pigment, they called this color *akase*, literally meaning "something that needs to be learned." This draws our attention to the fact that the eye initially does see, but that the conscious observation, the distinction brought about by giving it a name "has to be learned"; in other words, it is developing. In his study "The Development of the Sense of Color" in the study-series *Welt, Farbe und Mensch*, Hebing gives many examples and quotes the work of H. Magnus, which appeared as early as 1880.

6.2 The school sketches by Steiner as described by Fritz Weitmann

Following is a translation from a chapter of the book by Fritz Weitmann *Aus dem künstlerisched Unterricht der Waldorfschule, Malen und Zeichnen in der Oberstufe* (*The Painting Education of the Waldorf Schools: Painting and Drawing in High School*) published by the Pädagogische Forschungestelle beim Bund der Freien Waldorfschulen, Stuttgart, in 1981.

In this highly interesting work for the high school level, Weitmann not only gives examples from his experiences as secondary school painting and drawing teacher, he also provides us with an ample overview of the Steiner quotes of which he made use. The first section covers the curriculum; the second part of the book is dedicated to *impulses for art and recommendations* by Steiner for art education. In the second part Weitmann discusses Steiner's painting works, or rather, the directions Steiner supported with sketches by painting or drawing, including the large and small domes of the first Goetheanum. He provides a concise but very interesting summary of the sketches Steiner made as recommendations for painting education. Weitmann writes:

> With the founding of the Freie Waldorfschule in Stuttgart in 1919 and the school for continued education in Dornach in 1921, painting education had to be set up within the framework of these schools. There the artistic principles were to correspond with that of living art, keeping the age-group in mind. In connection with this, Steiner developed a series of pastel sketches as examples to help with the development of education.
>
> The first two sketches "sunrise" and "sunset" were created simultaneously. Both motifs are outwardly similar. They show the rising and setting sun above a flat horizon. Yet the color mood is different. The similarity in the composition invites the

spectator to find the difference in the pictorial mood. Of course this has been done deliberately. This contains the pedagogical, fertile element.

If each painting is considered individually, one may be uncertain whether it is a sunrise or sunset. In nature these can look very different; yet each sunrise and sunset have something in common, something typical at its foundation. Steiner gave himself the task to work this out in a pictorial way. When we look at the sketches simultaneously, the difference in mood becomes apparent. Yet not everyone can see the difference easily, because the difference is expressed in pure pictorial qualities rather than exaggeration. In the morning mood the sun enters the gates of the day in vermilion red. Blue-green nuances allow us to experience the cool and freshness of the morning. Clouds painted in yellow and reddish tones support the rising movement of the sun in both form and gesture. Contrastingly the evening mood shows warmer, yet more subdued colors. The orange of the sun has a matte quality, it has lost its radiating strength and appears to glow within itself under the descending cloud shapes. While the mood here encourages a reflection of the day that has been, the morning mood evokes action.

The rising and setting of the sun opens and closes the day and places boundaries around the night. In the alternating day and night the human feels part of the great breathing rhythm of the earth. He / she experiences his / her link with the cosmos. This relationship between earth and sun is also experienced in the paintings. The vertical rising and falling movement, together with the horizon line can become an invisible hieroglyphic, a cross described within the event.

The next two sketches, "trees under a sunny sky" and "trees in the storm," were also created simultaneously. They too have similar composition. As regards content, however, they are very different. They have been taken one step further in condensing the image. There is a clear progression from the first to the second sketch. The relationships between cosmos and earth are reinforced on the side of the cosmos, the unusually wide format of the sketch emphasizes earth's horizon. Also the movement in the sky, gathering into storm clouds, has been forced into a horizontal direction. The light of heaven is clouded over. Within this stormy landscape one can see a rhythmically positioned group of trees. The green areas of the foliage of the crown of the tree, the various directions of the reddish trunks and the shapes of the hill in saturated green together with the way in which the sky is painted, create a composition out of movement and tension.

On the subject "trees under a sunny sky" the soft green of the leaves appears free-floating in the clear blue of the sky. The red-brown of the trunks brings cheerful life. The latter was the starting point of the composition (so we have been told) which indicates that the composition aspect was given priority in this case.[34]

The sketch of "trees in the storm" is a conversion of the first. Because the atmosphere consists of gathering storm clouds, everything else is condensed in the process: the green of the trees, the color of the trunks and the color of the meadow below. The trees are included in the movement of the storm with their dark red trunks bent in one direction. The steel blue of the clouds dominates the obscured earthly green. A dramatically sombre mood has been created. The cosmic breathing rhythm of the earth is disturbed by the event, by gales and thunderstorms.

In the first pair of sketches the task is in working out the difference in color, in the second pair, the composition and

---

34. Marie Groddeck. *The Sketchbook of Rudolf Steiner* (not translated yet into English), Dornach: 1959.

the intensification of color. The law of polarity and *Steigerung* (enhancement) becomes clear.

We now arrive at the third pair of sketches "a sunlit tree by a waterfall" and "head study." The difference in subjects belies the fact that these sketches were also made simultaneously. Yet, one and the same motif connects them: the light. For the first time in these series the external light comes to the fore as a theme. Up until now the colorful mood of the painting had condensed itself to a tangible content. Now the process of becoming has progressed to such a degree that the objects in the depiction receive the light externally, that light and shadow explain themselves. Yet everything remains purely pictorial.

On the colored sketch "sunlit tree by a waterfall" one can see how the light flows towards a tree obliquely in green-yellow-black color nuances. On the other side a blue waterfall contrasts with the yellow flow of light in the composition. Between the tree and the waterfall is a space filled with water vapor and light with bluish yellow colors playing within it. The bottom in a strong brown carries the whole.

This color study is an image for the life of the elements. In all sorts of ways the elements meet and mingle in a free play of forces; they manipulate the prosperity of the tree, rooted in the earth. This magic mood could evoke fluttering butterflies, humming insects and singing birds. One can think of the activities of elemental beings in nature, the way they appear in myths and fairy tales.

According to Marie Groddeck, when demonstrating this sketch, Steiner began with the descending sunlight. He condensed it to a tree of light and flames, in which the earthly green was woven afterwards. The trunk, the most solid part, was the last to appear in contrast with the tree motifs discussed previously, where the trunks were the first to be drawn. This sketch is an excellent example to show what Steiner means by "bringing the observed color interplay in relation to the spiritual." The oblique light flowing into the space on the sketch cannot be observed in reality, however, it can be felt and experienced inwardly. It becomes visible only there where it touches matter. What is experienced inwardly is, however, no less real than what can be outwardly observed. The visible and invisible together provide an image of true reality. If we place the inner experience on the expressionist side, we have united this trend in both styles in the image. Steiner once said that a future painting style will be positioned between expressionism and impressionism.[35]

"Head study" takes us away from the nature motifs; for the first time a person becomes the motif. This study has been treated similarly to the tree motif. The subject is the light. A simple profile in yellowish-red nuances contrasts with a blue background. The delicate shadow areas clearly show how the face is connected to the light. Whereas the tree was created by condensing the light, the head space was left open. The blue background was done first, in which the profile was left open like a negative. The process of becoming was the initiative of the surroundings. In the "sunlit tree" sketch the process came from an inner impulse. Subsequently the illumined head was further developed with yellowish-orange tones.

Rudolf Steiner once demonstrated in one of his lectures, for those who "live" in the creative force of color, how two color patches, a yellow with a blue surround, are enough to recognize a head and profile. The way the radiating, fraying yellow and the bordering blue interact gives the impression that nose, eyes, mouth and chin are formed. He called this color setup "the basis for a face in profile." Encouraged by the "head study" later on,

35. See Steiner's *Art in the Light of Mystery Wisdom*, London: Rudolf Steiner Press, 1984.

colorful maps were made in geography on the same basis of color perspective.

The color study "mother and child" completes this series and is its climax. It contains a primordial human motif given form out of the color. This study is consequently very important, because Steiner explains every stage of its creation during the painting process. The stages in which the image was created simultaneously show the pupil's development in painting during the twelve year school plan. First, experiencing pure color within the soul, in increasingly richer nuances through which the child is guided in the first few years; finally, the more conscious form in painting and developing the qualities in painting in the higher classes. The artist Luise van Blommenstein, who attended this lesson, recorded this experience. We borrowed some of the characteristic details from her description.

Steiner had told the pupils that he wanted to show them a painting done "entirely out of the color," and he applied a soft, oblong vertical stroke in curved blue, and next to it a yellow patch on the stretched paper. He added: "As you can see, these are two entirely different colors, blue and yellow, but they are very compatible and pleasant to observe. Which other color would fit in?" He mixed a soft pink color out of various pastels and painted a small path next to the yellow. While turning to face the pupils he said: "These three colors together make a triad, as in music. It is a unity within itself. Now we want to paint the rest of the sheet, however. For this purpose we need to find a color not belonging to this triad at all." He applied a soft fresh green around the other colors. The entirety was intensified by a violet which connected with the blue at the bottom left. Steiner said: "Look here at the bottom right a little patch of white remains. Now we must fill up this space with one of the triad colors to keep it all together. Can you feel how this is necessary for the composition?" This was done in a soft blue. Then he carried on: "Right, we've finished that; now the sheet is full. That is a color symphony. That is beautiful in its own right. Now however, we'll see what we can make out of this. We'll paint something in the yellow. But yellow is yellow, one cannot see; so we need to add a little red."

Then we are told how he carefully carried on working, until eventually a face was created, to which he commented: "Those eyes you can just draw." He then drew a small head in the pink. "What else can we make from this? Let's say: "mother and child," but then we need a connection between mother and child." This connection was painted with a golden-orange for the arms and hands of mother and child. After some further development and harmonizing of the whole, he applied an illumining yellow from top to bottom over the background with broad brush strokes, changing the green into a golden mood. "The light comes from above, it should radiate ..."

In van Blommenstein's first description there is a faint echo of this mood during the painting hour and of the motif of this image. The painting came about in three clear stages: The first led to an experience in color-form, a triad; the second to the color richness of the composition: a color symphony; the third led to the creation of the image out of the color: the motif. The latter was not a starting point, but a result. From his experience of the color of the soul mood "motherly love," the image of the mother with the child was created. Steiner wanted to express motherly love, he said later. He had intended to execute this pastel study in watercolor, but unfortunately he did not. A large watercolor with this theme was created out of a different color mood and within a different context.

The motif of motherly love leads to a general love of humanity. Steiner had painted it as a central motif in the small dome—it formed itself into an image representative of humankind. We have not included the pastel sketch. It does not belong with the school sketches. This theme would be too demanding for the pupils.

This concludes the section by Fritz Weitmann. His book carries on with a description of Rudolf Steiner's training sketches for painters and includes large pastel sketches and watercolors. The connecting chapters "Goetheanum and the Bauhaus" and "The Question about the Creation in Form in Painting Art" are of importance for the secondary school teacher in particular, but also for a general understanding of Steiner's art impulse in our time.

Afterword

In the beginning of the book we started from the experience of color in our immediate environment. After the great journey through the multicolored curriculum and our reflections on color we return to this theme. Have these newly acquired insights changed our perception of nature? Have these sense impressions, supported by comprehensive thought processes developed an entirely new sense in us, a sense of art? And can we connect this sense to life itself in such a way that we can speak of "sense of life," life as an art? Steiner considers this and says that the force at the basis of this sense of art is love: love for fellow human beings and the surrounding world, a force that we can apply when working with children. Love, nourished by insights into humanity. Testing this knowledge with keen observation, in fact, renders each educational "system" superfluous: Love is education. After all the interaction between teacher and pupil is the most important, the most conclusive factor in the development of the child: The science of education becomes the art of education.[36]

Our intention is to place the painting curriculum within this context. An isolated painting lesson or exercise has no right to exist within a pedagogy constantly striving for renewal. These color

36. See Steiner's *Waldorf Education and Anthroposophy II*, GA 304A, New York, Anthroposophical Press, 1996, as well as *Education and Art* and *Education and the Moral Life*, London: Rudolf Steiner Press.

moments will become concrete if we can string these colorful beads onto a strong necklace. The thread keeps disappearing into the bead and is momentarily invisible. Reinforced with our experiences we should let go of our wish to have immediate results and standards. "Using the night" within this process has its special place "outside the teacher's efforts." We can only pick up the thread the next day, to carry on working on the necklace. Each spring we try to complete the necklace, in order to return to it the next school year, to expand it. This is how we create a piece of jewelery for life. Whoever wears it can travel richly through life and share a bead wherever necessary. Our wish is for this book to contribute to a long series of colorful beads, acquired in childhood and cherished as a precious possession in adulthood.

– Summer 2003

Bibliography

of Selected Titles in English

D'Herbois, L. Collot. *Color I & II*, Driebergen, Netherlands: Stichting Magenta, 1981.

Goethe, Johann Wolfgang von Goethe. *Theory of Colors*, Cambridge, MA, M.I.T. Press, 1976.

Hauschka, Magarethe. *Painting as an Exercise for Breathing*, Ann Stockton, translator, Boll/Göppingen, Germany, 1975.

Kandinsky, Wassily. *Concerning the Spiritual in Art*, New York: Wittenborn Art Books, 1976.

Lissau, Magda. *The Temperaments and the Arts*, Fair Oaks, CA: AWSNA Publications, 2003.

Mayer, Gladys. *Colors, A New Approach to Painting*, Hereford, England: Mercury Arts Group, 1983.

Merry, Eleanor C. *Art: Its Occult Basis and Healing Value*, London: New Knowledge Books, 1961.

Rosenkrantz, Arild. *A New Impulse in Art*, London: New Knowledge Books, 1967.

Schindler, Maria. *Goethe's Theory of Color*, London: New Knowledge Books, 1970.

Steiner, Rudolf. *Art as Seen in the Light of Mystery Wisdom*, London: Rudolf Steiner Press, 1984.

_____. *The Arts and Their Mission*, New York: Anthroposophic Press, 1964.

_____. *The Child's Changing Consciousness*, New York: Anthroposophical Press, GA 306, 1996.

_____. *Colour*, London: Rudolf Steiner Press, GA 623, three lectures, 1971.

_____. *Colour*, London: Rudolf Steiner Press, GA 291, twelve lectures, 2001.

_____. *Conferences with the Teachers of the Waldorf School in Stuttgart, Volumes, 1, 2, 3, 4,* Forest Row, UK: Steiner Schools Fellowship Publications, 1989.

_____. *The Education of the Child in the Light of Anthroposophy,* London: Rudolf Steiner Press, 1965.

_____. *The Evolution of the Earth and Man*, New York: Anthroposophic Press, 1987.

_____. *Four Temperaments*, New York: Anthroposophic Press, 1987.

_____. *Goethe's Conception of the World*, Spring Valley, NY: Mercury Press, GA 6, 1985.

_____. *Goethe's Standard of the Soul* (includes an English text of *The Green Snake and the Beautiful Lily),* New York: Anthroposophic Press, 1979.

_____. *How to Know Higher Worlds: A Modern Path of Initiation,* New York: Steiner Press, GA 10, 1993.

_____. *Man as Symphony of the Creative Word,* London: Rudolf Steiner Press, 1995.

_____. *Nature's Open Secret*, New York: Anthroposophic Press, GA 1, 2000.

_____. *Practical Advice to Teachers*, London: Rudolf Steiner Press, 1976.

_____. *The Riddle of the Soul*, Spring Valley, New York: Mercury Press, GA 170, 1996.

_____. *Soul Economy and Waldorf Education*, New York: Anthroposophic Press, GA 303, 1986.

_____. *The Spiritual Ground of Education*, New York: Steiner Books, 2003.

_____. *The Study of Man*, London: Rudolf Steiner Press, GA 293, 1966. Now published as *The Foundations of Human Experience*, New York: Steiner Books, 1996.

_____. *A Theory of Knowledge: Based on Goethe's World Conception*, New York: Anthroposophic Press, GA 2, 1968.

_____. *Theosophy*, New York: Anthroposophic Press, GA 9, 1994.

_____. *Ways to a New Style of Architecture*, GA 286, manuscript, 1982.

Stockmeyer, E.A. Karl. *Rudolf Steiner's Curriculum for Waldorf Schools I & II*, London: Rudolf Steiner Press, 1965.

Turgenieff, Assja. *The Imagery of the Goetheanum Windows*, London: Rudolf Steiner Press, 1976.

Printed in Great Britain
by Amazon

75791618R00122